More
Milledgeville
Memories

More
Milledgeville
Memories

Hugh T. Harrington

Charleston · London
History PRESS

Published by The History Press
Charleston, SC 29403
www.historypress.net

Copyright © 2006 by Hugh T. Harrington
All rights reserved

Cover image: General William T. Sherman. *Courtesy Library of Congress.*

First published 2006
Manufactured in the United Kingdom

ISBN-10 1.59629.192.3
ISBN-13 978.1.59629.192.8

Library of Congress Cataloging-in-Publication Data

Harrington, Hugh T.
  More Milledgeville memories / Hugh T. Harrington.
     p. cm.
  ISBN-13: 978-1-59629-192-8 (alk. paper)
  ISBN-10: 1-59629-192-3 (alk. paper)
  1. Milledgeville (Ga.)--History--Anecdotes. 2. Milledgeville
(Ga.)--Biography--Anecdotes. I. Title.
  F294.M6H36 2006
  975.8'573--dc22
                              2006025090

Notice: The information in this book is true and complete to the best of our knowledge. It is offered without guarantee on the part of the author or The History Press. The author and The History Press disclaim all liability in connection with the use of this book.

All rights reserved. No part of this book may be reproduced or transmitted in any form whatsoever without prior written permission from the publisher except in the case of brief quotations embodied in critical articles and reviews.

For Sue, who makes all things possible.

Contents

	Preface	9
	Acknowledgements	11
I	A Most Bizarre Investment	13
II	The Lady's Honor and an Early Grave	17
III	The Three-Eyed Man	23
IV	Hanged for Murder: Guilty or Innocent?	25
V	Thomas Johnson: Man of Many Wives	33
VI	The Assassination of Abner Zachry	35
VII	Immodest Young Women on Public Exhibition	39
VIII	The Axe Murder of Smithy Leonard	45
IX	A Unionist in Georgia	49
X	Secret Marriages	53
XI	Henry Denison: Lost Poet of Milledgeville	59
XII	The Asylum Rifle Team	63
XIII	The Drunken Duel	67
XIV	Sam Jemison: The Wild Child	73
XV	The Irrepressible General D.H. Hill	75
XVI	Dr. Lyell's Big Gully	81
XVII	The Cold Water Cure	83
XVIII	"Insane" Actor Murders: Was He Performing?	85
XIX	The Perils of Purloined Firewood	91
XX	Honor Restored Through Bloodshed	93
XXI	Moonshine and Murder	97
XXII	Mary Mapp's Revolutionary Dough Raiser	105

XXIII	Let There Be Light	107
XXIV	The Sacking of Westover Plantation	109
XXV	The Worst Christmas Milledgeville Ever Had	113
XXVI	Breaking the Chains of Legend	117
XXVII	Milledgeville Tunnel is Found!	119
	Index	123

Preface

My intention in writing this book, as with its predecessors *Remembering Milledgeville* and *Civil War Milledgeville*, is to tell history in a manner that will be accepted by the general reading public. I don't write for an audience of historians. I write for real people. These people have far too often been exposed to history in school by those who didn't like the subject and consequently taught it, through clenched teeth, to a class of near-comatose students.

History does not have to be taught that way. One does not need to burden history with memorization of precise dates, names and analytical arguments. The history-teaching professionals have failed millions of people by turning them off to history for life.

History *can* be interesting. It can be both entertaining as well as enlightening. The reader need not be assailed with pages of drudgery. Instead, history can be told as a series of stories or tales that feature real people, not abstract concepts—stories of people who face problems, make their choices and live with the consequences. Without fanfare the reader finds himself reading about the passions that cause crime, outcomes of jury trials and the lives, events and sometimes failures of long-forgotten individuals. Teaching through stories is as old or older than the Bible. I do not compare my humble scribbling with the Bible, of course, but one learns from the Bible that there is more in the telling of tales than mere tales.

If the reader chooses to embark on the venture, turn the pages and perhaps, just perhaps, awaken an interest in history that has been yearning to be found.

A brief word about sources of information. In almost every case, I have used the newspapers of the period, both local and surprisingly distant, for much of the factual material. I supplemented the newspapers with whatever primary sources were available. I avoided secondary sources as much as possible.

Hugh T. Harrington
Milledgeville, Georgia

Acknowledgements

When my previous Milledgeville history books appeared, I did not know what sort of reception they would receive. To my astonishment and delight, they have been warmly welcomed. My thanks and appreciation go to those readers locally and across the country who have taken the trouble to comment on the books.

I want to thank Judy Ennis Larson, Derek Veal and Elaine Ennis Williams for their help with the Ennis genealogy and the Ennis family's long-term involvement in Baldwin County. Alexa Filipowski Elliott provided information on Sam Jemison. Mark Dunkelman gave new insights into Sherman's March. Eileen Babb McAdams supplied many useful suggestions and obscure historical knowledge. Dorothy Haizlip Ward shared little known Zachry information. Encouragement and support came from many, including Jim Turner, director of the Old Governor's Mansion, Louise Horne, Betty Dawson, Floride Moore Gardner and David N. Wiggins, who also provided assistance with images.

Gail W. McDonald has enthusiastically supported my projects. Her personal expertise in local marketing and promotions has been extremely helpful.

Nancy Davis Bray, GCSU University archivist, and her staff unfailingly provided cheerful and professional assistance. Lillie E. Crowe, system director, Twin Lakes Library System, has acquired microfilms of nineteenth-century newspapers, which have been invaluable. In addition, Ms. Crowe has generously promoted my previous books at the library and made them available for purchase. Pam Beer welcomed my column, "'Round and About," which appears irregularly in the *Baldwin Bulletin*.

I especially want to thank my wife Sue for not only putting up with this book project but also for proofreading and correcting a multitude of grammatical errors. Without her stabilizing influence this book, and little else, would never become reality.

I

A Most Bizarre Investment

Solomon Smith was a lifelong actor and theater manager. In 1832 he was the manager of the theater in Milledgeville. One morning in the early fall he was lounging at his broker's office, smoking a cigar and discussing various investment opportunities when a "dandified individual" entered the office. This individual, who shall remain nameless, had a very high opinion of his own appearance. He wore multiple finger rings and a magnificent breast pin on his shirt. His coat and hat, vest and boots were tailor-made and a perfect fit. His kid gloves were spotlessly white. His hair was oiled and combed in the latest fashion. He also sported an enormous pair of whiskers.

The dandy joined the gentlemen in discussing various investment opportunities, stocks, land and commodities. At one point the dandy stated, "I will sell anything I've got, if I can make anything on it." One of the gentlemen replied, "Oh no, not anything. You wouldn't sell your whiskers!" The men thought that was a humorous comment and chuckled.

To their surprise, the dandy replied, "I would, but who would want them? Any person making the purchase would lose money by it." Sol Smith entered the conversation by saying, "I would be willing to take the speculation, if the price could be made reasonable."

The dandy, in good spirits, said, "I'll sell 'em for fifty dollars!" Smith replied, "Fifty dollars for both of them?" The dandy responded with a firm "Yes!"

"I'll take them. When can I have them?" replied Smith.

"Any time you choose or call for them."

"Very well. They're mine. I think I'll double my money on them, at least."

A bill of sale was drawn up stating, "Received of Solomon Smith fifty dollars in full for my crop of whiskers, to be worn and taken care of by me, and delivered to him when called for." The dandy signed it in front of the other gentlemen who acted as witnesses.

The dandy left the broker's office with fifty dollars in Central Bank of Georgia notes. He was soon telling all his acquaintances about the bargain he'd pulled off on old Solomon Smith. The men in the broker's office laughed and told Smith that he had lost his mind. Smith replied, "Let those laugh that win; I'll make a profit off those whiskers."

For over a month, whenever Smith and the dandy would meet, the dandy would ask if Smith wanted his whiskers. Smith would reply that he'd let him know and in the meantime the dandy was to take good care of them, including oiling them occasionally.

Everyone in town knew that the dandy had sold his whiskers. People would comment, "There goes the man with old Sol's whiskers!" It was a simpler age 175 years ago. People took pleasure in small things. Things like the fate of Solomon Smith's whiskers were the talk of the town.

After a couple of months the already large whiskers had grown considerably. The dandy could not trim them, as they were the property of Smith. A large and fancy ball was to be given to the members of the state legislature. Smith made some inquiries and determined that the dandy was to be one of the managers of the ball. The time had come to claim his whiskers.

The evening of the grand ball after the dandy had dressed for the occasion, Solomon Smith sent for the barber and for the dandy to join him at the broker's office. When the dandy entered the office he knew there was trouble brewing. The office was packed with spectators eager to see the barberous proceeding.

"Can't you wait until tomorrow? I have several ladies waiting for me to escort them to the ball," asked the dandy. Solomon Smith replied, "I don't see why you should wear *my* whiskers to the ball. Sit down, this will only take a minute."

After lathering his face the barber made a few strokes with his razor and half of the dandy's face was cleanshaven. "Come, come," said the dandy, "let the gentleman have his whiskers; he's impatient."

"Not at all," replied Smith, "I'm in no hurry myself. As I think of it, your time must be precious at this particular hour; I believe I'll not take the other whiskers at this time."

The spectators burst into uncontrolled laughter and applause. The dandy began to insist that Smith take all of his whiskers at once. However, Smith asserted his right to take his property when it suited him.

While he would not have used the term, the dandy was in a very "hairy" predicament, and he knew it. Over the roar of the near hysterical crowd he offered to buy the remaining whiskers back from Smith. First he offered ten dollars, then twenty, then thirty, then forty and finally fifty dollars. Solomon Smith was unmoved. He said he had bought the whiskers as an investment and wanted to make a profit as any good investor would. He would accept one hundred dollars and in exchange would return ownership of the remaining whiskers to the dandy.

The dandy paid the hundred dollars and went to the ball cleanshaven, much to the delight of the citizens of Milledgeville.

II

The Lady's Honor and an Early Grave

Much has been said about deeds that were done for the sake of a lady's honor. On the edges of the memory are vague recollections of formal duels and damsels in distress being rescued by knights in shining armor. More realistically, there were also encounters, frequently with tragic results, that took place among ordinary people, often among friends.

In Baldwin County, there occurred in 1892 and 1893 instances where the perceived or real threat to a lady's honor resulted in death. These cases and the legal outcomes provide a glimpse inside the minds of the participants and the juries.

The first example took place on the quiet Sunday afternoon of May 29, 1892, in the churchyard at Lingould's Chapel about four miles south of Milledgeville. The calm was interrupted by the firing of seven shots that left two men grievously wounded.

A young man, Charles Richardson, had recently been rejected as a suitor by Cora Barnes, the sister of Richardson's friend, William D. Barnes. The previous week Cora had married another man. As a reaction to the wedding, Richardson wore black crepe—as a sign of mourning—in his hatband. He also made some remarks that her brother took as offensive.

Barnes went looking for Richardson to resolve the matter. He found Richardson attending Sunday school at Lingould Chapel.

Barnes called him out and they walked into the churchyard, arguing in undertones. Suddenly, one of them shouted, "Then we will settle it here!" They both pulled revolvers and began firing. One witness said that Barnes hit Richardson with a stick as Richardson's revolver became entangled in his handkerchief while he was drawing it, thus enabling Barnes to get his own revolver into action.

It is uncertain who fired first. However, Barnes was hit twice, once in the shoulder and once in the side with the ball lodging next to his spine, causing paralysis. Richardson was hit in the right side with the ball lodging in the muscles of his back.

At first it appeared that both men would die from the exchange of gunfire. However, after a few weeks Richardson was healing. Barnes never regained consciousness, lingering for almost two months before dying on July 21. He was buried in Memory Hill Cemetery.

Immediately after the death of Barnes, Richardson was arrested for his murder. He was released in a few days after posting $2,000 bail.

Richardson was never brought to trial. The grand jury, meeting in September, returned a "no bill," thus ending the case. At the time, the newspapers referred to it as a "duel" although it was not a formal duel as we think of the term today. This was simply a fight between two men, former friends, over the perceived insult to one man's sister.

The following May a similar act of violence took place in an effort to protect the honor of a lady. In the small hamlet of Stevens Pottery in the southern part of Baldwin County, a young man named Daniel Gooden had for some time been making unkind remarks about the wife of another young man, David Upshaw.

On the afternoon of May 16, 1893, Upshaw could stand the remarks no longer. He took his double-barreled shotgun and went to Stevens Pottery in search of Daniel Gooden. Gooden was in the Pottery building. Upshaw waited on the porch for him to come out. As Gooden walked into the street, Upshaw came up behind him and, at about eight steps away, fired his shotgun at Gooden's back. Gooden turned after he was hit, and Upshaw fired the second barrel into Gooden's face before quietly walking away.

Daniel Gooden was carried to his house, where he died during the night. The coroner's jury held, "over his body," an inquest the day after the shooting at the home of Daniel Gooden. Several witnesses gave testimony.

The first witness was young Johnny Gooden, the nine-year-old son of the dead man. He had gone to town with his father to pick up the mail. He clearly saw his father shot in the back and then again in the face by Upshaw as he went from the Pottery office to the shop.

Another witness, Jack Scott, saw Gooden going from the Pottery office to the shop when David Upshaw shot him in the back with a "double barrel breech-loading shotgun." Gooden turned and "threw his hand to the place where he was shot and says, 'Oh, don't kill me,'" to which Upshaw replied, "God damn you," as he shot Gooden in the face. Upshaw then reloaded the shotgun and walked away.

Dr. Gilmore was called in to render assistance and reached the dying man about 11:00 p.m. He testified that Gooden's left eye was shot out and several shots had struck his face. The wound in the back, which the doctor did not think would have been fatal, was from his buttocks to his shoulders. The shotgun had been loaded with "small shot."

Lewis McCullar was able to shed some light on events that had preceded the shooting. In "early spring," David Upshaw and another man had come to ask McCullar's advice, saying that Gooden "had been using some bad language and telling scandalous tales about Upshaw's wife." McCullar referred Upshaw to a lawyer, who said that Upshaw could sue Gooden but "didn't think it would amount to much, and advised [Upshaw] not to spend any money on it." Upshaw told McCullar he could not stand to have a man talking about his wife in that way. Upshaw considered leaving the area. Upshaw asked McCullar to speak to Gooden and ask if he would "not make any more remarks about him or his wife." McCullar discussed this with Gooden, who agreed not to talk about Upshaw or Upshaw's wife in the future.

McCullar saw Upshaw on the Sunday preceding the shooting, and Upshaw told him that Gooden was still talking about his wife. Upshaw did not say what he was going to do but did say that he "couldn't put up with it."

McCullar was asked by Upshaw to go into town with him the morning of the shooting. On the way Upshaw never spoke of

Gooden. When they reached Stevens Pottery, Gooden walked past Upshaw, who said, "Dan, I suppose you have been talking about my wife again." Gooden made a reply that Lewis McCullar could not hear. McCullar said, "I thought Mr. Upshaw was going to shoot Gooden, and I walked off to keep from seeing it. I went in the house as soon as Upshaw and Gooden commenced talking."

W.E. Brown testified that a few days before the shooting Gooden had told him that he saw Mrs. Upshaw "and a man go into the bushes together, but would not tell the man's name." Brown told Upshaw what Gooden had said and Upshaw flew into "a heat of passion and said, 'God damn him! He had promised not to mention my or my wife's name any more.'"

The coroner's jury, after listening to this testimony, found that Gooden "came to his death by gunshot wound inflicted by David Upshaw and decide the same to be voluntary manslaughter." The following morning Upshaw turned himself in to the authorities in Milledgeville. He posted his bail and was released. His trial was scheduled for July.

The trial consumed two full days with evidence and argument: "Great interest was manifested in this remarkable case." A large crowd packed the courthouse anxious to hear the attorneys' arguments, which were "opened by the Solicitor General in his usual strong and forcible manner, followed by J.D. Howard, M.W. Hall and Joseph E. Pottle in able speeches for the defense [with] Robert Whitfield closing for the prosecution in a speech of wonderful power." It is not known what evidence was produced for the defense. Clearly there was ample evidence for the prosecution. The jury got the case on a Thursday evening and deliberated until Saturday morning but could not reach a verdict. The judge called in the jury, recharged them and sent them back to the jury room. They still failed to agree, and on Saturday afternoon the judge declared a mistrial.

At the next term of court the case was tried again. Again the trial took two days. At this trial the defense introduced no witnesses other than Upshaw. He testified simply that Gooden had persistently slandered his wife and he had killed him. The jury was out for only two hours before returning a verdict of not guilty.

It seems inconceivable that today a man could hope to get away with a killing where he intentionally sought out his victim and shot him in the back. A defense based solely on the shooter feeling the need to stop a man from making unkind, although perhaps true, comments about his wife would be grasping at straws. However, in 1890s Milledgeville, the honor of a lady—even a lady who may not have been honorable—carried a great deal of importance, not just with the men who defended her honor with a gun but also with the juries who passed judgment on her actions.

III

THE THREE-EYED MAN

IT'S NOT OFTEN THAT ONE gets the opportunity to view, up close and personal, a three-eyed man. This rare scientific curiosity came to Milledgeville on June 15, 1896, where he was to speak and be seen at the CME Church on Franklin Street. This church was located just west of where the main gates to Memory Hill Cemetery are today. Milledgevillians, never ones to miss out on educational prospects, were eager to see, to learn and to advance their own knowledge of nature and awaited the event with great anticipation.

As if a three-eyed man wasn't enough to bring out a crowd, this particular marvel was billed also as "part elephant and part man; in his mouth, on one side he had 48 teeth, and on the other side he had 24; nine ribs on one side and six on the other; that he could lift 1000 pounds from the ground." As is usual with spectacular attractions such as this, the subject had been closely studied by "noted physicians."

As an added bonus the three-eyed man would "tell the story of his life in the English and Mexican languages." It was standing room only in the church that hot summer evening. Admission was ten cents but those who wanted to get really close to the wonder of the world paid fifteen cents. After days of expectation, the great moment finally arrived.

The three-eyed man had a manager: Reverend M.E.H. Cordon of Washington, D.C., who had arrived in Milledgeville in time to preach a sermon at the church the day before the arrival of the three-eyed man. After the service Reverend Cordon invited the congregation to come to the church the following evening for what would certainly be the experience of a lifetime. The world may not have been prepared to learn the secrets of the three-eyed man but Milledgeville was.

The three-eyed man arrived on the Central Railroad train at 9:00 p.m. He was taken by hack to the church. There he sat mute, wrapped in a black cloth, while the assembled multitude sang, prayed and listened to Reverend Cordon speak about the three-eyed man. The big moment arrived and the three-eyed man spoke. Rather than speaking in English or Spanish, he only spoke in gibberish.

The pastor of the church, Reverend R.H. King, smelled a rat. He stood, interrupting the three-eyed man's gibberish, and announced to the crowd that he had been deceived. Reverend King said that the entrance fees should be returned to the people as the three-eyed man was a fraud. Someone shouted that the church could keep the money. Clearly, the patrons wanted to deal with the three-eyed man and Reverend Cordon in their own way.

A mass of humanity surged to the front, overwhelming the scientific curiosity and his associate. The dark cloth was torn away to reveal a black man partially wrapped in rubber cloth to appear like elephant's hide. A superficial search was made for the third eye but it was not located, to no one's surprise.

A melee followed in which the lights were extinguished, and the miscreants were propelled out the front door of the church where a woman armed with a broom began swatting the swindlers. Following her lead, the citizenry showered the former celebrities with blows to their heads and shoulders.

Breaking free, the two men fled north on Liberty Street. The three-eyed man proved there was nothing of the elephant about him. He was definitely fleet of foot as he was able to outdistance the howling mob that pursued him while shouting and firing pistols. The Reverend Cordon, who was not so quick, was overtaken and beaten again.

Apparently neither of the men was seriously injured. Wisely, they took the next train out of town. The Milledgeville citizenry proved, as they still do, that they were far too smart to be taken in by con men. To this day, not a single three-eyed man has again appeared in Milledgeville.

IV

HANGED FOR MURDER: GUILTY OR INNOCENT?

IN 1878 TWENTY-SIX-YEAR-OLD MICHAEL SHAW was hanged in Milledgeville for the April 30, 1877 brutal murder of his twenty-four-year-old wife, Ordeoro. Did the evidence support a conviction? While we do not have the benefit of trial testimony, we do have contemporary newspapers that give good accounts of the murder investigation and the events that transpired afterward, including the hanging. A review of the newspapers may leave some with a shadow of a doubt as to his guilt.

The initial article appeared the day after the crime, describing how Mrs. Shaw, living in the country eleven miles west of Milledgeville, "was murdered yesterday morning by two black fiends in human shape." The story was that Mike Shaw had left home in the morning to cut some firewood. He heard a gunshot at the house and returned to "find his wife lying at the door with her brains beaten in with a lightwood knot—her skull was broken in several places, also her arm and hand which she doubtless used to ward off the blows. By her side sat their blood splattered little daughter, 4 years of age, who said two black men had killed her mother." Mrs. Shaw was also shot in the head, presumably with Mr. Shaw's pistol, which was missing.

The neighbors were soon on the trail of the two mysterious black men. They found blood smears on a fence, which gave them the direction to search. However, the dogs they brought in to help were unsuccessful in finding a trail. Milledgeville's law enforcement officers picked up two "suspicious-looking negroes" and put them in jail, as they were "unable to give a satisfactory account of themselves."

Within a few days the focus of the investigation began to change dramatically. The first article in the *Union Recorder* had been written based on a report from a brother of Mike Shaw. The four-year-old child changed her story and said that her father, Mike Shaw, had killed her mother. Shaw's mother-in-law, Sarah Moore, strongly believed her daughter was murdered by Shaw and was pressing for prosecution. Rumors "of the most damaging kind" began to circulate about the area. It was remembered that Shaw had been arrested for the murder of a black man and for being a member of the Ku Klux Klan in 1875, but as he could not be positively identified, he was acquitted after being given a lecture by the judge. Now Shaw was arrested. The two black men were released from custody.

The newspapers gloried in graphic accounts of the crime. One carried headlines of "A Wife's Lost Life; A Hyena Husband Who Murders the Mother in the Presence of their Child; Deaf to the Pleadings of Love and Seared by the Contact of Sin; The Finding of the Dead Body Sweltering in a Pool of Blood; the Arrest of the Hardened Uxorcide Charged with the Dastardly Crime."

At his preliminary hearing, several people testified as to what they had witnessed. Dr. I.L. Harris had made the postmortem examination. He stated that the left side of the woman's head was badly bruised and gashed and that there was a hole in the top of her skull from a bullet. He also said that there were scratches on the face of Mike Shaw. The defense counsel objected to the testimony of the scratches, and it went in the record under protest.

Sarah Moore, the mother of the dead woman, testified that she heard a person scream twice the morning of the murder. Later, looking out from her house, she saw Shaw and his little daughter coming toward her house with blood on the daughter's cheeks and clothes. He told Mrs. Moore that his wife had been killed by someone and that the child said it was a Negro. Mrs. Moore said that there was "a bad state of feeling between Shaw and his wife."

A hired man, described as "a half witted sort of a man" who lived with the Shaws, David Butler, stated that he went out to plow and that Mike Shaw had gone out to cut logs. He heard a gun fired and Shaw yelled to him, asking where the firing had come from. Butler replied that it was from the direction of Shaw's house.

A Mrs. Butler, who was not the wife of the witness David Butler, testified that she had heard screaming and then a gunshot, then heard Mike Shaw call to David Butler. It was about a minute from the time of the screaming to the time Shaw called to Butler. She also said that just the week before the killing Mrs. Shaw had told her that she was on better terms with her husband than she had been for the previous twelve months.

Mike Shaw was sent to the jail in Richmond for safekeeping while awaiting his trial in August by the superior court.

The case against Shaw was based solely on circumstantial evidence and the prosecutors wanted more hard evidence before trial. They sent to Atlanta for Captain E.C. Murphy, who had a reputation for being a fine detective. Murphy spent several days in and around the area where the killing took place. Whisperings began that Shaw had been cruel to his wife and that he was a "terror to the neighborhood, especially the colored population, who regarded him as a Ku Klux. It was thought that some of the witnesses were afraid to testify against him." Shaw was suspected in the killing of several blacks and an anonymous note was received by a Colonel McCombs saying that the skeleton of a black man could be found in his well. A search of the well turned up the skeleton. One wonders who sent the letter to McCombs. It was said that Shaw was the leader of a local band of "desperate men" known as the "Georgia Tigers." No evidence surfaced to connect him with any of these activities but the rumors continued.

"Half witted" David Butler changed his story. At his own request he was locked in the county jail for his own protection after disclosing new information to Detective Murphy. He was released when arrangements were made for him to live in a different area. Detective Murphy returned to Atlanta, leaving the impression that the case against Shaw was now solid. Butler's changed testimony was that he saw Shaw beat his wife with the piece of wood then drag her into the house. He then heard gunshots from inside the house. Shaw emerged from the house and, seeing Butler, put a pistol to Butler's head and told him he would kill him if he ever told what he had seen.

The trial of Michael Shaw consumed two days, which was a long trial by the standards of the day. There was no direct evidence of Shaw's guilt other than the testimony of David Butler. David Butler was not an ideal witness for either the prosecution or the defense. As one of the supreme court justices later wrote after reviewing the case on appeal, "Besides contradicting what he had sworn to at the committing trial, he testified before the jury that he did not know what State he lived in, nor how many months are in a year, nor how many days there are in a week; also, that he could not count ten, and had never tried." Another supreme court justice wrote, "a fool is rarely a knave, and little children and fools are apt to tell the truth, because they have not the capacity to invent a lie, and this man's evidence impresses me, as it did the jury, that he told the truth like a child."

The jury returned the verdict that Shaw was guilty of murder. The judge pronounced sentence "that Shaw was to be taken to Fulton County jail for safe-keeping, and on the 12th day of October next to be returned to Baldwin County, and between the hours of 10 AM and 2 PM be hanged by the neck until he is dead, dead, dead," reported the *Union Recorder* of August 28, 1877, with dramatic finality. At the same time, Shaw was indicted for having murdered a black man by the name of James Bostwick, whose bones were found in McComb's old well near his residence.

On the night of October 2, Michael Shaw and another convicted murderer, Gus Johnson, cut through iron bars and then tunneled out of the Fulton County jail. Apparently they were the first to successfully make an escape from that facility. They were on the loose for several days before being apprehended near Powder Springs, northwest of Atlanta.

The *Atlanta Constitution*, in its retelling of the murder tale, added that Shaw had been tried in the past for beating his wife. Mrs. Moore, the murdered woman's mother, stated that her daughter had often told her that Shaw had threatened her life and that she was in constant dread of him. Physically, Shaw was described as having superhuman strength and also a "peculiarly brilliant and baleful eye—what is commonly called the 'snake eye.'"

Shaw's hanging was delayed as his attorneys took the case to the state supreme court in January of 1878. The case was delayed again and it was not until June that the supreme court decided against him. Shaw returned again to Baldwin County and was taken to the courthouse with the Baldwin Blues, the local militia unit, as escort.

The judge asked him if he had anything to say. Shaw replied, "Nothing more than I said before, that I have not had a fair trial." The death sentence was to be carried out on July 12, and the execution was ordered to be private.

Throughout the ordeal, Shaw was composed and displayed a courage that the newspaper reporters found "admirable," commenting, "Alas! that a man possessing these manly powers—this great physical courage—should not have the moral force to restrain his evil passions."

He was visited in the jail by his friends, attorneys, his mother and young daughter. He clarified what he meant by saying he was not getting a fair trial—that David Butler had sworn falsely against him. He proclaimed that he was innocent and had no confession to make.

Late in the same afternoon Shaw attempted suicide by taking strychnine that he had brought with him from Atlanta concealed in the binding of his Bible. He went into convulsions and doctors immediately came to his assistance. They told him that strychnine caused a very painful and horrible death whereupon he took the antidotes they had offered. He was returned to Atlanta to await the day of his execution.

Shaw's brother circulated a petition with many signatures to Governor Alfred H. Colquitt asking for a commutation of the sentence to life imprisonment. Some said that they "would not hang a dog on Butler's testimony." The petition was sent to the governor by Shaw's defense attorneys, DuBignon and Whitfield. The governor, however, refused to commute the sentence. The *Union Recorder* commented that "a large majority of our citizens never had any doubt of his guilt."

On July 1, one of the prosecuting attorneys, D.B. Sanford, received a warning: "I have been unhappily placed in a position to know there will be an effort to relieve the guard of Shaw on the railroad by parties that you least suspect. I would sign my name but it would place me in antagonism of my dark friends. Signed: A. Friend."

In response to this communication, the sheriff and three deputies went to Atlanta to pick up Shaw and did not disclose by which train they would be returning. No attempt was made to "relieve" them of Shaw. The Baldwin Blues guarded the jail during the night. Shaw was chained to the floor and two guards remained inside the cell with him.

A notice appeared in the July 9, 1878 *Union Recorder* over the name of Colonel Miller Grieve stating

> *The Cavalry are ordered to report to Captain Lattimer, immediately in front of the Capitol Building, on Friday, 12 July, at 10 o'clock precisely, armed with repeating pistols, loaded. The Infantry will receive their orders through Captain Herty, their commander. It may not be amiss to state that while I do not desire any unnecessary ostentation or display, yet it must be borne in mind that the business in hand is no child's play, and must be undertaken in earnest. To the furtherance of this end, it will be my endeavor to attach to it all the dignity that invariably belongs to all solemn and important decisions.*

Shaw was visited by three Catholic priests, who prayed with him. He talked with his guards but did not sleep. He refused requests by the press for interviews. Despite the pronouncement that the execution would be private, a huge crowd of three to five thousand filled Milledgeville for a chance to glimpse Shaw as he was taken to the gallows.

The gallows had been erected near the Oconee River bridge (south of the current location of the river bridge) with an eighteen-foot fence around it. At noon the sheriff took Shaw from the jail and placed him in a carriage for the half-mile ride to the river. He was escorted by the Baldwin Blues and fifty cavalrymen. Shaw rode in silence with his eyes on his open prayer book.

At the river he spoke to the crowd while standing in the carriage, saying, "I have nothing in the world against any man. The county officers have all been very kind to me, and I do not want my people to think hard of them. I have committed many great sins, but have prayed to God and do hope that he has forgiven me." He then recited the service that his spiritual advisors had arranged for him and entered the gallows enclosure.

He ascended the scaffold with a firm step and seemed to be absorbed. He prayed for fifteen minutes while standing on the trap with his hands and feet bound; his head was covered with a black hood; his neck placed in the noose. He asked the sheriff if he could have a few more minutes as he was "not ready yet," and the sheriff granted the request. He then said to Sheriff Obadiah Arnold, "Good-bye, tell your wife good-bye for me." He resumed his prayer and while the words, "O God have mercy" were on his lips, the trap opened and he dropped. His body "writhed fearfully" for several minutes and then a crucifix that he had been holding fell to the ground. After thirty-seven minutes the doctors pronounced him dead. Upon examination, they found that his neck had not broken: he had died from strangulation.

The *Union Recorder* made a point of saying that on the gallows Shaw never said that he was innocent. However, it should be pointed out that he never admitted guilt, either.

The day before his attempted suicide, Shaw wrote a letter to his mother. In it he asked his mother,

> *Take care of my baby and meet me in Heaven, for I feel that I am better off than the ones that has sworn my life away. Now I hope that those who has done all they can against me are satisfied. I don't want my friends to stop work until they find out the right party. It will be found out some day, when it is too late for me. I know my treatment and my wife's wishes, for I worked as hard for my wife as any man that ever lived, and I am as clear of my charge as a baby, and God that is in Heaven knows…Bury me by my wife, and baby if it is agreeable with all parties, if not agreeable with all parties suit yourself.*

The burial location of Michael Shaw is unknown; his body was shipped to Stevens Pottery in the southern part of Baldwin County. His wife is buried in West-Neal Cemetery, a small family cemetery off County Line Road in Baldwin County now grown up in brush, trees and vines. Her grave had been marked but is no longer visible. Her mother, Sarah Moore, who spoke out so strongly against Michael Shaw has a small simple gravestone. It reads, "Sarah Moore, born April 15, 1828. Died June 2, 1900, She Hath Done What She Could."

Was Mike Shaw guilty of the murder of his wife? Some will say he was. For others it is still an open question. One might question the weight put on the changeable testimony of the "half witted" David Butler and wonder if he was pressured by Shaw to make his first statement or by Detective Murphy to make his revised statement. There is also the question of Shaw's violent past and the rumors surrounding him, which may have been taken into consideration by the jury. Also, the story told by the four-year-old child is open to speculation. While there were no other viable suspects at whom to point a finger, there was little solid evidence to point at Shaw. So the questions will always remain: was Mike Shaw guilty of murder? Or was an innocent man hanged for a crime he did not commit?

V

Thomas Johnson: Man of Many Wives

It's not uncommon for a man to have more than one wife. I don't mean more than one wife at the same time but, rather, a succession of wives. Death or divorce can put a man into the market for a replacement wife. Usually, this sad situation happens only once or twice in the life of the unfortunate husband.

Not so with Thomas Johnson. Johnson may hold the record in Milledgeville for the largest number of women married to the same man. He had so many wives that somewhat incredibly the number he actually had is in doubt. More about that later.

Thomas Johnson was born in Virginia in 1800 and lived almost his entire life in Milledgeville. He was married several times and outlived each of his wives. In November of 1861, he enlisted as a private in Company F, Second Battalion of Georgia State Troops, becoming a rather elderly private at the age of sixty-one. He was discharged in April of 1862. But the old guy was determined to serve if his services were required. When he saw the Confederacy rocking and Sherman burning Atlanta, he decided to reenlist. In late October 1864, he enlisted as a private in Company G, Forty-fifth Georgia Infantry. He surrendered on April 9, 1865, at Appomattox.

Returning home to the misery of postwar Milledgeville, he worked to rebuild his life. At an age when men usually are content to sit on the porch or cracker barrel and reminisce about the achievements of youth, Johnson was active. Nothing could keep him down for long.

On March 20, 1875, after having put the war behind him, his settled life was disrupted again. This time it was not the storm of war, but rather a real tornado that interrupted his routine. His house was demolished by the tornado. His forty-five-year-old wife Mary Ann was "horribly mangled" and lived only a few hours. Mary was buried in Memory Hill Cemetery alongside his previous wives. No doubt Johnson was prostrate with grief over the tragic death of his wife.

Never one to let the grass grow underfoot or dwell on past adversities, the resilient Thomas Johnson began to rebuild his house right away. He was now seventy-five years old. He immediately realized there was something he needed besides a new house: he needed a new wife. Fortunately for him, he was vastly experienced in the art of replacing wives.

The citizens of Milledgeville speculated, and no doubt some wagered, on how long it would take for Johnson to find another bride. I suspect that few really appreciated the skills Johnson had acquired through many years and many successful courtships. He married his new wife, the pretty thirty-one-year-old Harriet Hemphill, on July 15, 1875, a mere 116 days after the tragic death of Mary Ann. One must admire the fast work of wooing and winning the young lady by the seventy-five-year-old Johnson.

We now come to the tricky question of just how many wives Johnson had. When he married Harriet Hemphill, she was referred to in the newspapers as his sixth wife. When he died in October of 1886, his obituary said that he had had six wives, the sixth surviving him. However, little more than a month later, a reporter from the *Atlanta Constitution* rambled through Memory Hill cemetery with a guide and wrote about the notable graves that he had seen. To our consternation, he describes Johnson's lot as containing the mounded graves of Johnson and seven wives. He added that a "lovelorn widow survived him." Regrettably, the names of the wives have not been discovered, so we are unable to determine if Harriet Hemphill was the "lovelorn widow" or if there were other wives after her.

We are left with the perplexing problem of the often married—and indefatigable—Thomas Johnson, the husband of six, seven or even eight wives.

VI

THE ASSASSINATION OF ABNER ZACHRY

A MILE SOUTH OF THE Morgan County line, on Georgia 441 in Putnam County, is a small family cemetery. One of the gravestones there is for Captain Abner R. Zachry and reads that he was "cruelly assassinated in Morgan County, December 17, 1896." Who was Abner Zachry and why was he cruelly assassinated?

Abner Zachry was born in rural Putnam County June 6, 1841. His father died two years later. Abner was brought up on the farm of his mother and stepfather. He attended the local Putnam County schools.

At the age of nineteen, in 1860, he had inherited from his father's estate assets worth $20,000. He was attending school at that time. A year later Abner enlisted in the Confederate army as a corporal in Company G, Twelfth Georgia Infantry. By July 1864, he had been promoted several times and was a captain. He had also been wounded three times. The most severe, a chest wound, was received at Fort Stevens, outside Washington, D.C. He was captured and taken to various hospitals and prisons, including the Old Capitol Prison in Washington. He is described in a prison document as having blue eyes and standing 6 feet 4½ inches tall. He was eventually released in June 1865 after the war had ended.

Returning to Putnam County, Abner Zachry married nineteen-year-old Eugenia Lyle in January 1866. He was a successful farmer. However, in January 1885, a few days after giving birth, his wife died. Abner now had to care for the newborn, Eugenia, and six other children, the oldest being his sixteen-year-old daughter, Lilla.

Lilla assumed the responsibilities of caring for her siblings. She was assisted by fifteen-year-old Hattie. The other children included the baby, two-year-old Abner, five-year-old Percy, seven-year-old Bertie and nine-year-old Guy. Lilla shouldered the responsibilities, conscientiously looked after the children and ran the household.

Thirteen months later Abner, now forty-four, married thirty-six-year-old Martha Singleton. Martha, known as Mattie, had been the children's schoolteacher. Lillie was apparently resentful that she was thrust aside, with her duties taken over by her stepmother. Lilla never accepted Mattie as her stepmother.

This uncomfortable situation was exacerbated five years later when Hattie married and moved to a new home on a farm a few miles from that of the Zachrys. She had been Lilla's close friend and confidante.

The uneasy truce between Lilla and Mattie continued for another five years while Abner Zachry continued to prosper. He became one of the wealthiest men in the county. However, everything would change on the evening of December 17, 1896.

Abner Zachry and Mattie were alone sitting by the fireside that cold and rainy evening. The children, with the exceptions of Guy and Bertie, were in the next room playing cards. Guy and Bertie were in a buggy on their way to a party in the nearby town of Godfrey.

A neighbor boy named Frank Durden stopped in to visit. When he entered the room, he looked at Percy and said that he thought he had just seen him outside the house. At that moment two gunshots were fired almost simultaneously in the next room where Abner and Mattie had been sitting. The children dashed into the room and saw through the acrid black powder smoke their father lying on the floor with a grievous wound to his head.

Sixteen-year-old Percy ran outside because the shots had been fired through the window. He found no one. Mattie struggled with the near-lifeless body of Abner to get it onto a bed. Meanwhile, farmhands rushed to the home of Hattie and also to locate Bertie and Guy. Hattie was home but her husband was out possum hunting. Bertie and Guy were located on the road in their buggy. Before they could arrive, Abner died without regaining consciousness.

The authorities had few clues to work with in their attempts to solve the murder. Rain during the night had obliterated any trace of the killer. It was determined that the fatal wound had been caused by two shots from an old-fashioned muzzle-loading shotgun. Along with the shot, brown paper wadding was found in the wound and in the room. Interestingly, and perhaps importantly, Mattie had been next to Abner and moved just as the shots were fired through the window.

Newspapers carried the story with dramatic headlines of "That Foul Deed, The Assassination of Capt. Zachry," and "His Head Shot Off." The story was the same in all of them. Abner Zachry had no known enemies and was apparently popular. There was no real evidence to point to a killer. One unfortunate black man named Judge Perryman was arrested solely because he was seen carrying a muzzle-loading shotgun and used brown paper as wadding for his charges. No case against Perryman, who said he was on good terms with Zachry, could be made; he was released.

When Captain Abner Zachry was laid to rest on December 19, the funeral was attended by many friends, former comrades in arms and of course the family. Or at least most of the family. Conspicuous by her absence was his wife. Mattie had taken her eight-year-old son, Robert, and a wagonload of possessions to her family home in Eatonton. She left the children of Abner Zachry a note saying that she had never been treated right by them and could not live with them after the death of her husband. She would soon move to Waycross, Georgia, where she would spend the rest of her life.

Lilla, now twenty-eight years old, again took on the role of "mother" for the younger children. The older boys ran the farm. Eventually, all the children married, except Lilla. She moved in with her sister Hattie and helped mother another generation of children. She lived until December 13, 1931, almost thirty-five years to the day after her father's violent death.

Neither a motive nor any real evidence was ever uncovered. No one was ever tried for the murder. It has been suggested that perhaps Mattie Zachry was the real target and that Abner had been struck unintentionally as Mattie had moved just prior to the shooting. However, there seems to be no motive for killing Mattie.

Her stepchildren were not fond of her, but it seems unlikely that they would have conspired to have her killed. Also, she could have been killed at a time or place that would not have endangered Abner.

    The unsolved murder has been long forgotten. The last child of Abner Zachry, young Robert who was taken to Eatonton after the shooting by Mattie, died in 1955. Few people stop at the little cemetery alongside the busy highway. Those that do will always wonder about the mysterious death of Abner Zachry, who was "cruelly assassinated" so long ago.

VII

IMMODEST YOUNG WOMEN ON PUBLIC EXHIBITION

With the onset of the Civil War, Southern women flocked to the Cause and formed a myriad of organizations to aid the soldiers in the field. Whether they were called the "Ladies Aid Society," "Soldiers Relief Society" or some other name, their missions were similar. A cottage industry was organized to manufacture all manner of uniforms, clothing, bandages and rifle cartridges. The ladies also raised money for various projects from funding the building of gunboats to buying food. Sometimes these money-raising ventures doubled as entertainment for the soldiers and citizenry. Concerts, poetry reading and singing were popular.

Women of every age group participated in these activities. In fact, almost every woman, from teenagers to beyond middle age, participated to some degree in a patriotic organization. Many devoted very long hours to the projects.

After three and a half years of these activities, the public displays by the talented young ladies of Milledgeville came under attack in the press. On October 18, 1864, a letter to the editor, signed anonymously with the name "Hope," was published in the *Confederate Union*. Hope, who claimed to be a Confederate soldier from Milledgeville, questioned whether it was appropriate "for young ladies to appear in public on the stage." Hope claimed that by performing on the stage a "gradual, almost imperceptible influence steals over the soul…destroying, or at least searing the finer feelings of her nature."

Hope asserted "that time and again have the fair daughters… charmed us with their delightful concerts. Yes, and from most patriotic, Christian motives. They were given superintended too, by noble women. The end, however, does not always justify the means." He continued, "Ye, who are to be the mothers of our rising, beloved Confederacy—ye who are to be our wives, are injuring yourselves. Let us raise the money in some other way, and cultivate, by every means possible, true modesty, delicate sensibility in our women. Do not supply my wants by robbing woman's soul."

He added, "I pledge my life, my heart, my soul to my wife, but give me, oh give me a true woman, a woman of fine feeling, of delicate modesty. How selfish we are, delightfully entertained by the concert, the pictures are beautiful, the music so sweet, we forget at what terrible cost."

Hope concluded by saying that he did not care for a show "where the first daughters of the community will be upon public exhibition—where they are applauded, jeered, whistled at."

In the same newspaper the editor commented that "our friend" Hope is "too hard on the young ladies."

> *The young ladies who took part in the concerts we have had in Milledgeville during the War, did so from patriotic and charitable motives and noble impulses, and but for the rudeness of bad boys, and uncultivated young men, who disturb the proceedings with whistling, loud talking and boisterous laughter, these entertainments would be altogether as unexceptionable as a select musical soiree at a private house. If all the bad boys could be kept out, and all the gabbing and silly young men could be taught propriety, the young ladies who participate in the concerts would not have their modesty in any wise impaired by appearing in public on the stage.*

The editor appears to think that the "bad boys," since they have not been kept out, have in some ways impaired the modesty of the young ladies. To some extent he agrees with Hope's position.

The October 25 edition of the newspaper brought a reply from Hope, in which he states that any public exhibition by a young lady is wrong. He contends that the "rude conduct of certain young men and boys" is inexcusable but that "appearing on the stage before a promiscuous crowd, although the most perfect order be preserved, exerts a baneful influence on a young girl."

Hope's first letter ignited long and laboriously argued replies from readers. One writer, who signed himself as "Soldier," commended the ladies, young and old, who since the beginning of the war "have rendered their name immortal by their noble fortitude, their deeds of charity and their acts of kindness to our suffering soldiers."

Soldier maintained that the young ladies "have cheered us on by their smiles and hearty assistance, to a more determined resistance to a hated and cruel foe: and in a word, they have been to us a perfect bulwark, an army of defense. Without them, and without their help, our ship of State would have stranded long ago, and our fair land would have been a waste, fit asylum for hooting owls and beasts of prey."

"An irremediable evil, and inherent in society," Soldier wrote, "...and foul blot upon society's fair form will appear. Boys will be bad, and young men will be silly, and in the great drama of life, in which we are all actors, we must, at times, expect to be 'laughed, jeered and whistled at,' for it is an evil of which we cannot rid the world." Soldier believed that the young ladies' "action, instead of unfitting them for society, has a tendency to do away with false modesty, and fit them to grace the parlor, and enable them to appear to better advantage in their association with the sterner sex."

Soldier concluded by writing, "I bid you, then, young ladies of Milledgeville, to continue in well doing, and not permit yourselves to be influenced by the squeamish notions of o'er sensitive persons."

Another correspondent, using the name "Caution," turned the tables on Hope. Caution warned that Hope "is not alone in this feeling of a necessity for 'humbly suggesting' improvements in the practices of others. Many may be found in New England of similar propensities—and the result of the exercise of this Puritanical desire to correct the errors of others, has been to deluge our land in blood, and carry an anguish to every heart in the land, thus calling upon our women to relieve the suffering by every means in their power—even to 'appearing on the stage.'"

Caution suggests that "instead of condemning a good institution because of some evils let Hope endeavor to prevent the 'jeers and whistling' of the boys, and other improprieties, at the next concert by the ladies, and if he and other objectors will exert themselves in the right way, these disagreeable features will disappear, and, while great good will be achieved, there will be no cause to deplore the attainting of the souls of the young ladies."

A letter from one of the young lady performers, who signed herself "one of the Milledgeville Show Girls," put Hope in his place in no uncertain terms, writing that Hope's "conclusions were unwarrantable, his insinuations ungentlemanly and his remarks wholly uncalled for." Show Girl also wrote she was

> *educated to feel that any display of woman's charms for the sake of admiration was as revolting as wrong. I have never followed the fashion of the day in a public exhibition of myself on the stage in the reading of composition at the annual commencement of a College, nor publicly sung at concerts of the same, and yet I have sung repeatedly that my fare-footed countryman might have shoes to cover his feet while fighting for my liberties, and feel no other glow mantling my cheek from the announcement, than that of pride that I have been able to add my mite in the furtherance of the cause.*

Show Girl continues, "I am conscious of no such 'gradual imperceptible influence stealing over my soul,' but every day the greatness of the work to which the women of the South are consecrated, viz: the nursing of the sick and wounded, clothing of the soldier in the field, and raising of funds to relieve the thousands destitute of our own sex exiled from home, makes me willing to bear the censure of the few, who like Hope punctiliously fear the 'injury' to my soul."

Going on the attack, Show Girl writes, "I will not ask why Hope is at home but I must think he would be better employed at the front than in newspaper scribbling impeaching the motives of those who in their limited sphere are endeavoring to deserve the highest encomium 'she hath done what she could.'"

The angry Show Girl wrote, "for fear he might again have his fine sensibility shocked we give him timely warning not to be present at our concert next week." Show Girl puts the last nail in Hope's coffin by ending her letter with her wish that Hope "will never be disgraced by a union with one of the Milledgeville Show Girls."

The November 1, 1864 *Confederate Union* carried the announcement that "A Concert will take place tonight at Newell Hall [located on the east side of the 100 block of South Wayne Street, approximately where Bayne's Army Store is located in 2006] under the direction of Mrs. Dr. Mitchell and Mrs. Moffett who will be assisted by the young ladies of the city, Mr. W.H. Barnes, and other amateurs. We can assure the public that this concert will be deserving, in every respect, of a liberal patronage. We hope that those whose business it is to preserve order, will see that no disturbance occurs. The concert will be repeated on Thursday night."

Three weeks later, the army of General William T. Sherman would be pouring through Milledgeville on its March to the Sea. The arguments about the propriety of concerts featuring young ladies were replaced by the urgency of mere survival.

VIII

THE AXE MURDER OF SMITHY LEONARD

Having written in the past about local nineteenth-century murders, I am sometimes asked by my more ghoulish readers about the most heinous of these crimes. While Milledgeville cannot, fortunately, boast of having had a Jack the Ripper–type crime spree, we have had the occasional sensational murder.

Perhaps it was Lizzie Borden, immortalized by the famous poem, who gave axe murders their grisly fascination.

> *Lizzie Borden took an axe*
> *And gave her mother forty whacks.*
> *And when she saw what she had done,*
> *She gave her father forty-one.*

The murder of Lizzie Borden's parents occurred on August 4, 1892. While it does not have the notoriety of the Lizzie Borden murders, the axe murder of Smithy Ennis Leonard took place over four months earlier on March 23, 1892.

Smithy Leonard was the sixty-year-old wife of Reverend Simeon C. Leonard, the pastor of Black Springs Baptist Church. Reverend Leonard said he returned home late in the afternoon from a visit to a neighbor to find his wife lying in a pool of blood. She was still living but unconscious. The house was ransacked during the apparent robbery but nothing was found to be missing.

Dr. Owen F. Moran was summoned to the scene. His examination showed that Mrs. Leonard had been struck six or seven times on the head with an axe. One arm was bruised when apparently she had tried to defend herself from the vicious blows. Mrs. Leonard never regained consciousness and died the following evening.

The Leonards' nephew, Sheriff C.W. Ennis, headed up the criminal investigation. The neighborhood was alarmed and searchers fanned out looking for the culprit who presumably was covered in blood from his horrific deed. Reverend Leonard said he remembered seeing a black man leave the house as he approached on the afternoon of the murder. He thought the man was a local woodcutter who sometimes supplied wood to the Leonards.

Ben Gause, the coroner, conducted an investigation into the cause of death. The coroner's jury, made up of J.B. Chandler, T.J. Croley, C.H. Babb, J.W. Champion, R.T. Harris and W.F. Howell, determined that "death was caused from wounds made with an axe in the hands of parties unknown to us and we, the jury, pronounce it murder."

Despite the energetic efforts of Sheriff Ennis and the neighbors, the murderer was not found. Governor W.J. Northen issued a proclamation on April 23 offering a reward of $300 for the "apprehension and delivery of said unknown murderer, or murderers, with evidence sufficient to convict."

The woodcutter, Lewis Williams, was arrested on suspicion and put in jail. However, there was no evidence to support charges and he was released. George Boykin, a black man seen in the area and described as a tramp, was arrested at the train station in Haddock. Another man, Alfred Greene, was also arrested.

In September, the superior court convened in Baldwin County. The grand jury released both Boykin and Greene when it found insufficient evidence to indict them.

Thirteen months after the murder, Reverend Leonard died at the age of sixty-nine and was buried at Black Springs Baptist Church next to his wife. The mysterious murder of Smithy Leonard was never solved.

Lizzie Borden, despite the famous poem, was acquitted at trial of murder. One of the strongest pieces of evidence on her behalf was that, despite the bloody murder scene, her clothing was blood free. It may be that the murderer of Mrs. Leonard also found a way to keep from becoming tainted with the evidence of his crime.

The murder of Smithy Leonard may not have gone unpunished, however. Four years and two days later, on May 25, 1896, a family at Gaithersburg, Maryland, was assaulted in their home and a young child was killed. A suspect, Sydney Randolph, was arrested for the crime. He was being held in the Rockville, Maryland jail for the grand jury when a mob of thirty to forty men came to the jail at 1:30 the morning of July 5. The prisoner was taken from the jail and hanged.

The news report stated that the mob "composed of the best citizens of the community, who were perfectly sober and orderly, quietly dispersed believing they had executed the perpetrator of the most atrocious crime ever committed in this county."

Shortly before the lynching a letter was received by the sheriff in Maryland from the superior court in Baldwin County. The court wanted to know if the man in custody, Sydney Randolph, "has a scar on either side of his face near the eye." It seems that the Baldwin authorities were looking for a man named Ben Temple, who had such scars, and suspected that he might have been the man apprehended in Maryland using a different name.

Randolph was examined and found to have the identifying scars. What evidence existed to connect Ben Temple with the Smithy Leonard murder is unclear. Whether this man, using the names of Temple and Randolph, was guilty of the Smithy Leonard murder will never be known.

IX

A Unionist in Georgia

The decision to secede from the Union was not an easy one to make. The citizens of Georgia were evenly divided between supporting Secession and wanting to stay within the United States. Some sections of the state were more Secessionist or more Unionist than others. Delegates were elected from each county to attend the Secession Convention in Milledgeville, the state capital. Some of the delegates were Secessionist, others Unionist and some undecided. Emotions ran high.

The convention in January 1861 ended with a vote for Secession. While many rejoiced, others were deeply troubled. A few months later, when open warfare broke out, most Georgians supported the war effort. However, there were some who strongly believed in maintaining the Union. Most of these people kept their thoughts to themselves as they did not want to be considered enemies by their neighbors or the Georgia or Confederate authorities. Some, like William A. Batson, did not keep quiet.

The U.S. government established a program in 1871 for compensation to Union sympathizers in the South who lost property due to the military action of U.S. troops. To qualify for compensation from the Southern Claims Commission the applicant filled out a form answering eighty questions, provided written descriptions of their losses and provided affidavits from witnesses. Tabitha Batson, William's widow, filed claim number 4170, which provides a good description of her losses in animals and foodstuffs to Brigadier General Judson Kilpatrick's cavalry in November 1864. It also provides information about the Union sentiments of herself and her husband as well as details about the murder of her husband that resulted from his vocal pro-Union stance.

When war came, Batson was age thirty-four, a respected justice of the peace and prosperous farmer with a wife and six children. He had a lot to lose. Before Secession he was outspoken in his position to remain loyal to the Union. After Secession, he was just as outspoken, only now he referred to his Confederate neighbors as "Rebels."

Batson and his family lived an isolated life in the southern part of Baldwin County below Scottsboro. Tabitha was estranged from her family in nearby Wilkinson County. Her two brothers were in the Confederate army. She did not see them before they left for the war and had no contact with them during the war. The neighbors, even friendly neighbors, did not want to associate with the Batson family as they did not want to be perceived as having Union sympathies even if their beliefs were similar to the Batsons'.

In the normal course of farm business, when William Batson would go to a store or other place where men gathered he would naturally come into contact with those who would speak of politics and the course of the war. Batson was very vocal in his dislike of the Confederate government in Richmond and the government of Governor Brown in Georgia. This caused heated arguments, and on at least some occasions fistfights were narrowly avoided.

Tabitha was as strongly pro-Union as her husband. In her affidavit she stated, "He nor I never done anything against the Union cause" and that "I was in favor of the Union all the time. My husband told me he voted against secession." She, of course, could not vote.

Unlike most women in the South, Tabitha swore that she "never belonged to any sewing society made no clothing for Confederate soldiers, or their families nor assisted in making none nor flags, nor military equipment nor prepare and nor furnished supplies for military the militia or soldiers."

During the first part of the war, Batson's views may not have been liked by many, but he actually had not crossed the line and become any sort of criminal. Initially, he was too old to be drafted. Later, when manpower shortages changed the requirements, he was forced to enlist in a militia unit. According to Tabitha, "He was forced into the militia a few weeks. He played off sick and would not go back."

Martin Hubbard stated in his affidavit that William Batson

> *was opposed to Secession and voted against Secession he talked against the war too much so for his good. He said a good deal. I have known men to get mad with him once he and I was at Scottsboro he got into an argument with N.K. Carnes.* [A man] *was speaking of what great things that the Confederates was doing this was the time that* [Confederate General John B.] *Hood* or [Confederate General Joseph E.] *Johnston was at Atlanta and Batson said that if fire was coming on him he did not want a man to tell him that all was safe and calm until he would get burned up.* [A man] *spoke up and I'll be damned but you are against us and the Confederacy? Batson replied he was. They came near having a difficulty this was only one month or so before he was killed.*

Hubbard continued, "His public reputation was that he was opposed to Secession and the War. I talked often with him. I heard J.N. Combes talk of him as a Union Man...He was killed by Bynum an enlisting officer," according to Hubbard.

J.N. Combes testified that Batson "voted against Secession and was an outspoken Union man. He said he did not intend to go to the War to serve against the Union army and if he ever did it would be when he was forced to do so and [he did not] intend to be forced." Combes remembered Batson "talking against the war and refusing to go when he was called, that was the reason that he was killed." Combes continued, "He would not fight for the Confederacy he said that the Confederacy was wrong and he did not intend to go to the war. That they would have to drag him before he would go. That was his last words to me this was about one week before he was killed. He was killed because he was so out spoken against the war and would not go to it he was Bush Whacked."

Just what happened when Batson was killed is unclear. According to Tabitha,

> *My husband was killed because he refused to serve in the army by a man named Byron a conscript officer. I was told Byron was the name of the person who killed my husband. He came after my husband and on a previous occasion. Dave Bowing was the only one that I knew. They asked me where my husband was. I told them I did not know where he was. They said if they could not get the Squire (my husband was a justice of the peace) they would take his fine horses. I said that they had no right to take his horses. They went off through the field to look for my husband and fired a gun to scare me as I supposed. There was 22 of them, they did not all come in the house. This was only a short while before my husband was killed…my husband would keep out of the way when any came about.*

The October 18, 1864 *Southern Recorder* reported that "William Batson, a magistrate in the Scottsboro district in this county, who having refused to go into the military service was last week shot by the arresting officer and died on Saturday last."

William A. Batson, a man with the courage of his convictions, died on October 15, 1864, eight days before his thirteenth wedding anniversary. Six months later the war was over. He is believed to be buried in an unmarked grave in the abandoned Batson Cemetery off the east side of Highway 243, south of Scottsboro.

X

Secret Marriages

Nearly everyone at one time or another gets married. The event can be huge, large or even small. I find the best marriages, however, are those done in secret. Anyone can have a wedding with lots of guests, a wedding cake and all the trappings of a traditional marriage. Those who seek—or find themselves forced to seek—private marriages come away with something far more memorable than just another wedding.

Dumas-Lawrence

Early on a Friday afternoon in August 1902, Pearl Dumas and Jefferson Lawrence determined that it was a good day to be married. Young Pearl was a clerk at the Joseph Dry Goods store. She worked through the afternoon as usual. At 6:00 p.m. she closed the store and, accompanied by two friends, went to the north gate of Georgia Military College. There, she found Jefferson Lawrence and the Reverend D.W. Brannen waiting for her. In the western archway of the GMC gate, Pearl and Jefferson were married.

The marriage was a complete surprise to their friends and families. The bride, described as a "bright and attractive young lady," was twenty-one years old. Jefferson Lawrence was thirty and the manager of a local farm. They enjoyed life together for fifty-six years until Jefferson died.

Bloodworth-Ivey

In June of 1896, a wedding took place in Milledgeville that was a bit more circumspect. Twenty-four-year-old Jim Ivey faced a problem. He and Sallie Belle Bloodworth wanted to get married but her parents objected. They had nothing against Jim, but they were so fond of their nineteen-year-old daughter that they didn't want her marrying anyone. Rather than trying to change her parents' minds the couple pursued their own line of action.

Accompanied by her brother, Sallie Belle came to Milledgeville to attend the commencement exercises at Middle Georgia Military & Agricultural College (now GMC). Jim Ivey met her in Milledgeville and they decided that their wedding day had arrived. Their friend Ben Finney was told of their plans and asked to get a marriage license and the services of a minister. A few hours later they, along with some close friends, met at the home of another friend, Mr. Bayne, where the Reverend J.A. Wray conducted the marriage service.

Sallie Belle's brother was not one of the witnesses to the wedding. He was informed after the fact as he was preparing to return home. It was his duty to report the marriage of his sister to his parents. Unfortunately, there is no record of what Sallie Belle's parents had to say when they were informed of their daughter's marriage. I trust that they got used to the idea. Jim Ivey became a prosperous young farmer known for his excellent character.

Miller-Ratteree

Uncooperative parents frequently engage in a losing battle when they try to prevent the marriages of their children. The young couples, when faced with obstacles, usually demonstrate that there is more than one way to skin a cat.

During the winter of 1894, Ada, the fifteen-year-old daughter of Robert Miller of Moseleyville (near the present Georgia War Veterans Home), wanted to marry a young man who worked on her father's farm. This young man, named Ratteree, was not approved of by the Millers. When they realized that an elopement was a real possibility they forbade her from seeing Ratteree and locked her in her room. Ratteree was ordered off the premises.

The best laid plans and schemes of well-meaning parents, however, are sometimes easily overcome. In June, Ratteree appeared at the Miller residence and demanded his wife. "His wife?" gasped the Millers. Three months earlier, on a trip to visit relatives in Wilkinson County, Ada and Ratteree had been married. Early the next morning Mr. and Mrs. Ratteree left in a one-horse wagon for Atlanta.

WHITE-HARPER

Occasionally, there are more than just protective parents who need to be circumvented. In 1901, one of the most strictly regulated girls' schools in the country was Georgia Normal and Industrial College (GNIC). Almost equally restricted was Georgia Military College (GMC). However, through a combination of detailed planning and bold action, these institutions as well as disapproving parents were no match for a couple wanting to marry.

Pretty sixteen-year-old Johnnie White from Laurens County was a student at GNIC. George Harper was a junior at GMC. One Friday evening in May, Johnnie slipped out of Atkinson Hall unobserved by matrons, teachers and housekeepers. She met George, who was waiting for her, on Hancock Street. They took the 8:00 p.m. train to Macon, where they arrived at 9:25. They took a cab to the home of an ordinary to get their marriage license. They then drove to the residence of Reverend W.W. Pinson, the pastor of the Mulberry Street Methodist Church. In his parlor, with both students wearing their school uniforms, he performed the marriage ceremony at 10:30 p.m. Mr. and Mrs. Harper then went to the Brown House Hotel for the night.

They spent Saturday in Macon. On Sunday evening, they took the Georgia Central through Milledgeville, passing a cheering crowd of their friends, as they went on to Meriwether. In Meriwether was George's father, W.I. Harper. He had no choice but to accept the fact that his son was married. He may have been shocked, surprised or even angry. However, one would like to think that he got over it before too long.

Harper-Wilson

In June Harper was in for another jolt. J. Herty Wilson, son of postmaster Carlos Wilson, announced that he and fifteen-year-old Claude Harper, W.I. Harper's second daughter, had been married since January 26. On that winter afternoon Herty Wilson had ostensibly gone for a ride with Claude Harper. But, unknown to their friends and family, they had gone to the Scottsboro home of John G. Thomas, justice of the peace, where they were married. They returned to their homes as if nothing had happened. They managed to keep their marriage a secret for four months. Now, however, Wilson was claiming his bride.

Hines-Reid

When planning a secret wedding, it is wise to have alternative plans in case of pursuit. George Reid had anticipated trouble and his foresight paid off. In late November 1901, he and Beulah Hines had surreptitiously left Milledgeville in a carriage. George had arranged for the marriage license secretly in Madison, as Beulah's brother was the ordinary in Baldwin County. They made their way to Meriwether, where they intended to take the train on to Eatonton to be married. Fearing pursuit, George stationed a friend on the train as it left Milledgeville. The friend was to signal George from the train if the plan had been discovered and pursuers were aboard the train.

Concealed near the station at Meriwether, George and Beulah waited for the train. It slowly came into sight but their friend was giving the danger signal. They allowed the train to continue on to Eatonton. Undeterred, George and Beulah continued on in the carriage with only a slight change in plans. Instead of getting married in Eatonton, they stopped at the home of John Bagley, justice of the peace, and were married by him.

Married, they proceeded on their way to Eatonton. When they entered the Eatonton Hotel, they were confronted by Beulah's brother. Outsmarted, he could only offer his congratulations to the resourceful newlyweds.

XI

Henry Denison: Lost Poet of Milledgeville

On the west side of Memory Hill Cemetery next to ten box-type vaults, there is a bronze marker with the curious wording "Graves of ten former members of the Georgia State Legislature." It is comforting to know that these long-dead politicians are not the current members of our legislature. Perhaps the writer was pulling our legs a bit. In any case, despite the bronze marker, there are only nine members of the legislature buried there. The tenth man is Henry Denison, who was not a politician.

Denison died from fever on October 31, 1819, at the age of twenty-three. Those few who know his name locally remember him as the first partner of Richard M. Orme. Orme had worked in the printing office of Seaton and Fleming Grantland, publishers of the *Georgia Journal* newspaper. Denison was a Milledgeville schoolteacher. Together, these men were to have been the founders of a new newspaper, the *Southern Recorder*. They ordered the equipment and materials needed to publish the paper, but before the first issue was published on February 15, 1820, Denison died.

Denison's gravestone gives some genealogy and information about his life. The epitaph reads:

> *Beneath this tablet reposes all that is mortal of* Henry Denison, *who died in Milledgeville, Georgia, October 31, 1819, son*

of the Honorable Gilbert Denison, and Huldah, his wife, of Brattleborough, Vermont. Reader, art though a Parent? Think upon thy own offspring; and sympathize with them; art thou a good Son? Mingle thy tears with his Parents; for he was the best of Sons; A brother? Mourn, for he was the kindest of Brothers; A Friend? Sorrow, for he was the firmest of Friends; Does the Muse inspire thee? Grieve, for he was of thy kindred; Art thou all that is manly and upright? Bemoan his early fate, for he was thy companion; But if though art a Christian, Rejoice—for Henry "is not dead, but sleepeth."

To mention the high qualities of the dead was common. But, there is something mentioned in the epitaph that gives us a clue about Henry Denison. "Does the Muse inspire thee? Grieve, for he was of thy kindred." Could Denison have been a poet?

In fact, he was a poet. Henry Denison was born in Guilford, Vermont, on May 31, 1796. As it says on his gravestone he was the son of Judge Gilbert and Huldah Denison. Perhaps in an effort to please his parents he entered the University of Vermont in November 1812 to study law. However, the institution was occupied by federal troops while the War of 1812 was in progress. He then went to Williamstown College, now known as Williams College. He eventually joined a law firm in New York City. He wrote a friend that law "is not altogether that dry thing in which light I had always been accustomed to view it." However, he could not escape the desire to write poetry.

In the winter of 1816–1817, he abandoned law and sailed from New York to Savannah. In the winter of 1818, he moved to Milledgeville, where he became a teacher. He also became good friends with Richard M. Orme. There is some indication that, for a very short time just before his death in October 31, 1819, he produced a weekly literary journal called the *Georgia Republican.* The *Augusta Chronicle* of September 24, 1819, carries an advertisement announcing that the first issue of the *Georgia Republican* would be published on the second Tuesday of September (September 13) by Walter Jones and Henry Denison. No copies of that publication are known to exist.

After his death, his friend Israel K. Tefft, the editor of the *Savannah Georgian*, wrote the epitaph that appears on Denison's gravestone. A few years later, Tefft collected Denison's poems and sent them to a publisher in Scotland. After many delays, a small portion of Denison's works were published in 1828, along with those of other American poets, in a small book entitled *The Columbian Lyre*.

Denison was not immediately forgotten in Milledgeville. Thirty-five years later, his friend and partner, Richard Orme, would still point out his grave and remark upon Denison's genius and character. Orme died in 1869 and was buried only twenty yards away from the friend of his youth. With the passing of Orme, the memory of Henry Denison was lost in Milledgeville.

In Vermont, Denison is remembered and considered a Vermont poet. This probably would surprise Henry Denison because in his poem "Woodville," he says in part:

> *But Georgia's clime delights me more;*
> *I would not journey north again,*
> *For all that art and nature pour*
> *Upon the fruitful land of Penn;*
> *For Nature's choicest bounty lies*
> *Beneath the warmth of southern skies,*
> *Here all the sweets of earth combine—*
> *Land of the orange and the pine.*

So, while Henry Denison is forgotten and lost among the former Georgia state legislators in Memory Hill, perhaps on cold winter nights in Vermont there are people who huddle around the fire and read Denison's poetry.

XII

The Asylum Rifle Team

Target rifle shooting was a very popular sport in the United States from the early 1800s until about World War I. Surprisingly, it was a spectator sport as well as a participants' sport. Huge crowds would go to the shooting ranges to watch their favorite competitors shoot even though it was impossible to see the bullets' hits on the targets. The scores, however, would be posted so the spectators would know how individuals or teams were performing.

The most famous of these shooting ranges was "Creed's Farm" or "Creed's Moor" on Long Island, New York. The facility soon became universally known as "Creedmoor." It was located just 15 miles east of New York City. The firing line was 570 feet wide and the range was 1,200 yards long. The first international match, between an American team and an Irish team, was held there in 1874. The match attracted a crowd of 8,000 spectators. The Long Island Railroad put in a station at Creedmoor to handle the large number of fans.

The rifles used by target shooters were not ordinary rifles that would be used by the military or hunters. They were mostly single-shot designs fitted with the latest delicate and precise sights. The triggers were so light that a mere touch of the finger would fire the rifle. The rifles were designed and balanced specifically for target shooting. Among the rifles used were those made by Ballard, Colt, Remington and Winchester. These single purpose target rifles were expensive. As a result, target shooting was a sport enjoyed by some of the more well-to-do gentlemen of the community.

Target shooting has had a long history in Milledgeville. The first recorded match took place in 1818. That match was between gentlemen from Baldwin County against a team from Jones County. Each man put up $500. This amount is equal to about $5,500 in today's dollars. Clearly, these men had confidence in their shooting abilities.

By 1886, target shooting continued to appeal to the prominent and wealthy citizens of the county, although no mention was made of wagering at these events. The Georgia Lunatic Asylum employees made up the Asylum Rifle Team. The team included Thomas H. DeSaussure, Dr. James M. Whitaker, Samuel A. Cook, W.B. Harper, Dr. Lodrick M. Jones, Dr. Iverson Harris Hall, P.A. West, O.C. Summers, Robert Augustus Stembridge, Stephen E. Wright, Augustus H. Russell, W.T. Wilson and Sidney J. Stembridge.

They tested their skills against the Milledgeville Rifle Team, which consisted of Dr. Iverson L. Harris Jr., George Caraker, S. Marshal, Mayor Sam Walker, George Whilden, Frank B. Mapp, Solomon Barrett, the postmaster Carlos Wilson, Howard Tinsley, Chauncey M. Wright, Charles L. Case, Herman Gumm, George Case and Dr. Callaway.

In one match between these two teams, held at a shooting range located somewhere on the asylum grounds, the distance was one hundred yards and the target a sixteen-inch diameter piece of iron. Each man would shoot five shots. The score was determined by the number of inches each shot was from the center of the target. The best possible score would be the lowest number of total inches. This type of scoring was known as "string measure."

In the first round, ten of the contestants missed the entire target. Among the best shots was one 3½ inches from the center and the worst, of those hitting the plate, was 8 inches from center. Scores on the next four rounds were considerably better. No doubt the competitors' nerves settled down as the contest continued.

The best score of the match was shot by W.T. Wilson with 12½ inches total string measure for his five shots. That's excellent shooting by any standards. Solomon Barrett came in last with a measurement of 50 inches.

The men, many of whom were former Confederate soldiers, clearly were having a good time as they decided they'd shoot another match of three shots each. The sole Union veteran, Carlos Wilson, the postmaster and former bugler of the Second Michigan Cavalry, came in first with a string measure of 6¾ inches. Dr. Jones was second with 9½ inches and Steve Wright had 10 inches for third place. Dr. Iverson Harris, despite having the steady hands of a surgeon, shot 24¾ inches. The worst score of 30, indicating he missed the target each time, was held by Robert Stembridge.

At the end of the day the total scores gave the victory to the Asylum Rifle Team with a total combined measurement of 151¼ inches, overwhelming the Milledgeville Rifle Team's 212¾ inches. A good time was had by all and future contests were planned.

At the next meeting of the rifle teams, the range was on Mayor Walker's pasture that was near his fishpond. This pasture was west of Flagg Chapel Church on Franklin Street. This time, instead of using "string measure," they used a more conventional target with a five-inch bull's-eye and scoring rings around the bull's-eye.

This match ended with a total score of forty-six for the Milledgeville team and forty-five for the Asylum Rifle Team. No doubt this victory, slim though it was, made the men of the asylum very concerned about the outcome of future matches. However, they assured the Milledgeville team that they would make a comeback as the target rifles they had ordered several months previously should be arriving soon. They hoped that shooting their own rifles would give better scores than borrowing rifles on the day of the match.

In the months that followed I am sure that the gentlemen of the asylum spent their spare time at the asylum range practicing with their new rifles for the next meeting with the team from Milledgeville.

Fifteen years later, a group of fourteen young women calling themselves the "Sharpshooters" organized into a rifle club. One of the elder members, at age twenty-seven, Sara Eva Perry was elected president. Mamie L. Roberts was the secretary and treasurer. The ladies purchased only one rifle and each contributed their own ammunition. They met each Wednesday afternoon at Tomlinson Fort Newell's to practice.

The other members of the Sharpshooters were Dorothy Newell, Nan Barksdale, Edith Carr, Gertrude Whitaker, Mary Newell, Lily

Prosser, Mattie Moore, Rosa Whitaker, Maybelle Moore, Marie Whitaker, Mae Allen and, perhaps the youngest, eighteen-year-old Mary Cline.

Unfortunately, while Dorothy Newell and Nan Barksdale were acknowledged to be accomplished shooters, scores and the results of any competitions are not available.

XIII

The Drunken Duel

When drunk, people do stupid things, and Joe Ewalt was drunk. About 7:00 p.m. on Tuesday evening, March 24, 1896, Ewalt and his friend Charlie Mathis had been playing pool and drinking at Charles Whelan's saloon on Hancock Street. What happened next is somewhat unclear. The incident is not only dimmed with the passage of over a hundred years but is told as though seen through a drunken fog by the only witness, Charlie Mathis.

Ewalt and Mathis approached the bar where their friend Walter Hemphill was working as bartender. Ewalt asked Hemphill for the return of a pistol he had earlier pawned for sixty cents. It is not known what model pistol this was, but it obviously wasn't a fine example of the gunmaker's art as sixty cents would amount to just over thirteen dollars in today's currency. However, it was enough of a weapon to ruin more than one life.

Hemphill told Ewalt that he couldn't return the pistol until the sixty cents was paid. Ewalt replied that another employee, a Mr. Brake, had told him he could have the pistol back if he promised to pay the sixty cents on Saturday. Obligingly, Hemphill handed the pistol to Ewalt.

Suddenly and unexpectedly, the scene escalated to a tragic climax. Mathis tells a very peculiar tale. According to Mathis, after handing the pistol to Ewalt, Hemphill walked down the counter and took proprietor Mr. Whelan's pistol from a drawer saying, "Yours isn't the only pistol in the world." Hemphill, however, made no threatening gestures or comments. Mathis, using the logic only a drunk would understand, then got the bright idea of suggesting Hemphill and Ewalt fight a duel. Next Mathis, apparently in a spirit of fun, said, "OK, you've both got your pistols, now do your shooting. I'll do the counting. One. Two. Three." At the count of three, Ewalt fired three shots into a very surprised Hemphill.

"My God, Joe, you have shot me. I thought you had better sense. What did you shoot me for?" gasped Hemphill. He then put Whelan's pistol back in the drawer. Hearing the shots, people rushed to the scene. Hemphill was laid down in the back room while medical help was summoned. A Dr. Croley and Dr. Winfield Robison arrived and rendered what aid they could. Mathis sat up all night with his wounded friend. Deputy Sheriff Perry arrested Joe Ewalt at the scene without incident.

The following morning Hemphill was taken to the residence of his father-in-law, C.A. Jones, where he fought for his life. With a bullet and rib fragments through his right lung there was no hope. Four days later, the twenty-two-year-old Hemphill died with his wife of three years by his side. Besides a grieving young widow he left a two-year-old daughter.

Hemphill's funeral was held at his home with the service conducted by Reverend J.A. Wray. He is buried in Memory Hill Cemetery in an unmarked grave at an unknown location.

At the coroner's inquest it was determined that Ewalt and Mathis had been drinking beer, but no whiskey, during the afternoon. The young men also did not appear to be badly intoxicated. At the age of twenty-three, Joe Ewalt found himself in jail, charged with murder. He hired local attorney Robert Whitfield to defend him. Ewalt received help from an unexpected source. The Honorable William C.P. Breckinridge, of Kentucky, wrote Ewalt offering to help with the defense.

Breckinridge, a lawyer, had been a colonel in the Confederate army and was now a former Congressman about to run for Congress again. Ewalt's father had been a close friend as well as an officer under Breckinridge. The Ewalts were a prominent family in Kentucky, and Breckinridge volunteered to do whatever he could to help the son of his old friend. Breckinridge's defense work in this unusual case would also bring a great deal of publicity that was politically desirable.

Colonel Breckinridge, "the silver tongued orator," had a very strong reputation as a speaker. His involvement created even more interest in this already interesting case. Lawyers and prominent politicians from all over Georgia converged on Milledgeville for the privilege of witnessing Breckinridge in action.

The trial attracted a huge crowd in what is now called the Old Courthouse in Milledgeville. Literally not another soul could be wedged into the building. People filled the aisles, the windows, hung on the railings of the bar itself and even sat on the steps of the judge's stand.

Milledgeville, always taking the lead in technology, put up a telephone-like contraption with a large funnel to pick up the sounds in the courtroom. It was placed in front of the speakers as they addressed the jury. The sound was apparently amplified so people crammed into other parts of the building could hear the trial.

As it was the middle of July, the temperature in the courtroom was unbearably high. The intense heat, however, did not discourage the throng. They were eager to hear the famous Kentuckian try to find some reasonable defense for the apparently senseless shooting of young Hemphill.

The jurors were D.H. Wilkinson, J.T. Hughes, Ben D. Myrick, Benjamin A. Bass, W.J. Green, C.L. Ivey, Thomas Prosser, L.F. Palmer, H.T. Bothwell, Forest Dunn, Daniel Brewer and I.C. Hudson.

The defense team took the approach that Ewalt was considerably under the influence of whiskey and that he accidentally fired the three shots that killed Hemphill. They also wanted to show that Ewalt and Hemphill were friends in an effort to show that there was no motive for Ewalt to have killed Hemphill.

Late in the afternoon of Friday, July 17, while giving his final hours-long summation to the jury, Colonel Breckinridge came close to passing out from the heat. He staggered to a table for support. The judge ordered a recess until 7:30 p.m. Unlike modern trials, recesses and adjournments were rare. The legal process was hammered through until a verdict was reached.

That evening, having recovered his strength, Breckinridge spoke to the jury for another hour and a half. According to the *Atlanta*

Constitution, Breckinridge's summation was "full of pathos and visibly affected the vast audience." He concluded at 9:15 p.m.

The prosecution's final argument lasted two hours. It was now 11:15 p.m. The judge's charge to the jury took only ten minutes. The jury had the choice of convicting Ewalt for murder or an acquittal. At 11:25 p.m. the jury was sent to the jury room to decide Ewalt's fate.

At 3:20 a.m. on Saturday morning, court was called back into session as the jury had reached a verdict: "We the jury find the Defendant guilty and recommend him to the penitentiary for life."

Ewalt's attorneys immediately made a motion for a new trial. They based their motion on the fact that the judge had not instructed the jury as to the law on involuntary manslaughter. Unlike today, the appeals process was swift. The judge, several weeks later after considering the motion, denied the request for a new trial.

The defense attorneys then appealed to the state supreme court. The high court denied the appeal a month later by stating,

> *The evidence showing conclusively and beyond doubt that the accused intentionally and without provocation or justification shot at the deceased three times with a pistol, each shot taking effect, and the facts admitted by the accused in his statement, notwithstanding a naked assertion therein that the killing was accidental, showing that the homicide was committed as above stated, a charge to the effect that if the killing was the result of accident or misfortune the homicide was excusable, was more favorable to the accused than he had any right to demand, and the court's omission to define what would constitute accident or misfortune affords the accused no cause of complaint.*

Joe Ewalt, at the age of twenty-three, was doomed to spend the rest of his life in confinement. Or was he?

A mere four years later the prison commission recommended to Governor Allen D. Candler that Ewalt be pardoned. He had been serving his sentence at the state prison farm. Ewalt was, according to the *Atlanta Constitution,* in a "drunken stupor" when he killed Hemphill and "the chances were that he did not know what he was doing." The newspaper went on to report that "Ewalt is the son of good Kentucky parents, had a good character previous to his crime and recently his health has failed. Mercy in his behalf was asked by a large number of citizens, including the solicitor general and eleven of the jury by which he was tried."

The governor pardoned Joe Ewalt in August 1902. One wonders if the family of Walter Hemphill thought justice had been served.

XIV

Sam Jemison: The Wild Child

Born in May of 1852, Samuel Jemison was too young to participate in the Civil War. His older brothers, Edwin and Robert, however, were soldiers of the Confederacy. A hundred years after the war, the haunting photograph of Edwin, killed in 1862, gained worldwide attention that it still enjoys.

Sam Jemison, though born in Louisiana, spent much of his childhood alternating between Louisiana and Georgia. Being a grandson of Milledgeville's prominent Baradel Stubbs, he was given a good education. In his teens he was sent to Washington College, now Washington and Lee University, in Lexington, Virginia. There, he was noticed by the college president, General Robert E. Lee, who wrote Sam's father describing Sam's achievements.

In 1872, after attending Washington College, Sam went to Monroe, Louisiana, where he studied law. Before being admitted to the bar in 1875, Sam dabbled in other ventures. He was the city editor of the *Macon Telegraph* and also the editor for the *Morning Star*, which did not succeed. He joined his father in his law practice, and when his father died Sam became city attorney of Macon, where he established a fine reputation.

In 1881, he was elected to the Georgia legislature. At the age of thirty-one, he clearly was a promising young man with a future ahead of him. However, there was something of a wild streak in Sam. It cannot be said that he courted danger or violence. However, violence seemed to swirl around him to a very unhealthy extent.

In 1878, at the age of twenty-six, Sam was attending an event when suddenly a young man started waving a pistol and firing at people in the crowd. He leveled his revolver at Sam and fired—a miss. He did not have the opportunity to fire another shot as Sam pulled out his own revolver and shot him dead. Only after the smoke cleared was it learned that the man had been firing blanks.

Two years later, shortly before midnight, Sam was standing in front of a saloon in Macon talking with some acquaintances. A man, known to Sam but clearly not a friend, walked up to him and started a political argument. He called Sam a liar and struck him with his fist. This man then pulled out a revolver and fired, severely wounding Sam in the chest and both legs. Despite his own wounds, Sam returned fire and injured his assailant.

A year before his death in 1886, Sam became involved in his last gunfight. He was at Benner's restaurant in Macon when he was approached by a man named Edward Stroenecker. At a distance of three feet, Stroenecker drew his revolver and started to fire at Sam. Sam stumbled to his feet while pulling his own revolver. The confrontation ended after four shots had been fired and both men were on the floor. Stroenecker was dead and Sam was critically wounded and not expected to live. Apparently Stroenecker had earlier asked Sam for a loan of some money. Sam had refused.

After many months, Sam recovered and was able to return to the courtroom and practice his trade. At the time it was thought that overwork may have contributed to Sam's death in December of 1886, at the age of thirty-four. It seems far more likely that his death was a result of his lifestyle, which included far too many gunshot wounds.

Sam Jemison is buried in Memory Hill Cemetery.

XV

THE IRREPRESSIBLE GENERAL D.H. HILL

COLLEGE PRESIDENTS COME IN ALL SORTS—from meek, mild academic types to strictly business administrators and the flamboyant, self-promoting incompetents. Few, however, could bring to the position such vast educational experience, battlefield skill and personality quirks as the colorful Daniel Harvey Hill. In 1885 he was appointed president of Middle Georgia Military and Agricultural College (MGM&AC), what we now know as Georgia Military College (GMC).

Daniel Harvey Hill, called "Harvey" by his friends, is remembered today as a general in the Confederate army during the Civil War. However, he was not hired as president of MGM&AC because of his military background but rather because he brought to the school an in-depth familiarity with education from both before and after the war.

He was born in the Upcountry of South Carolina in 1821 to devoutly Presbyterian parents. The family regularly read the Bible aloud. He was intensely religious and held strong Puritan beliefs—much as did Stonewall Jackson. (General Jackson, incidentally, was married to the sister of Hill's wife.) Hill wrote at least two religious books, *A Consideration of the Sermon on the Mount* in 1858 and *The Crucifixion of Christ* in 1859.

The ancestors of both Hill and his wife were Patriots during the American Revolution. That family history played a part in Hill's view of his role in society. The family tradition of fighting tyranny during the Revolutionary War continued with his own very strong political beliefs. As did many others of his day he saw the actions and attitudes of the South before the Civil War as a "Second American Revolution."

In a speech before the Davidson College Board of Trustees on February 28, 1855, Hill described his own love of South Carolina in terms that tell a great deal about his character. He said, "This love [of South Carolina] has only been strengthened by the abuse she has received from abolitionists, fools and false-hearted southrons. I pride myself upon nothing so much as having never permitted to pass, unrebuked, a slighting remark upon the glorious State that gave me being." Throughout his life, Hill would never be reluctant to say, very bluntly, exactly what he thought. His prickly personality often got him into trouble with his superiors.

It would not be an overstatement to say that Harvey Hill was outspoken in the extreme. It's not just anyone who can write a textbook on algebra and fill it with politics and anti-Northern prejudices. His book, *The Elements of Algebra*, published in 1857, contains some very surprising mathematical problems for the student.

Three examples are:

A Yankee mixes a certain number of wooden nutmegs, which cost him ¼ cent apiece, with a quantity of real nutmegs, worth 4 cents apiece, and sells the whole assortment for $44; and gains $3.75 by the fraud. How many wooden nutmegs were there?

The field of battle at Buena Vista [Mexican War] *is six and a half miles from Saltilla. Two Indiana volunteers run away from the field of battle at the same time; one ran half a mile per hour faster than the other and reached Saltilla 5 minutes and 54 seconds sooner than the other. Required their respective rates of travel.*

A man in Cincinnati purchased 10,000 pounds of bad pork, at one cent per pound, and paid so much per pound to put it through a chemical process by which it would appear sound, and then

> *sold it at an advanced price, clearing $450 by the fraud. The price at which he sold the pork per pound, multiplied by the cost per pound of the chemical process, was three cents. Required the price at which he sold it, and the cost of the chemical process.*

Looking beyond the difficulty of the problems, one is struck immediately by the implications that Northerners are cheats and cowards. This was Hill's belief and he saw no reason why it shouldn't be part of the lesson for the students. Hill, teaching at Davidson College at the time, asked a fellow faculty member to read the manuscript of the book. The colleague was shocked by what he had presumed would simply be an algebra book. He told Hill that many would find the references offensive as they clearly involved sectional prejudice. Hill responded that he didn't care whether the book was received favorably in the North or not. It was what he believed; so he would write it in his own way.

As a young man Hill received an appointment to West Point. He graduated twenty-eighth in a class of fifty-six in the year 1842. His lowest grades were in mathematics, yet later in life he became a mathematics professor.

During the Mexican War, Hill gained the reputation as a fighter. He personally led storming parties at the battles of Padierna and Chapultepec. He gained fame within the military and in South Carolina for his bravery and leadership.

Resigning from the U.S. Army in 1849, Hill joined the faculty at Washington College in Lexington, Virginia. Later, after the Civil War, Robert E. Lee would become president of this small college, and the name would evolve into Washington and Lee University.

While at Washington College, Hill was held in very high regard as a teacher by the student body. A student recalled him as being "strictly impartial and very generous in recognizing and encouraging any originality and unusual ability" in his students. It was also said that he "had the rare capacity of interesting his pupils and of compelling them to use their faculties, often it seems unconsciously, in a manner that surprised themselves."

In 1853 Hill was invited to become a professor of mathematics at Davidson College. It seems that the Board of Trustees considered the president weak and hoped that Hill's forthright style might help quell an unruly student population that was disturbing both the college and the surrounding community.

It was a situation that sounds very familiar, with the students, many of whom were considered out of control, involved in heavy drinking and loud carousing late into the night. Their nightly extravagances often included violence. Hill decided that students had been "allowed to trample upon all laws, human and divine" and that they were of an "undisciplined mind, and uncultivated heart, yet with exalted ideas of personal dignity, and a scowling contempt for lawful authority, and wholesome restraint."

Hill was not interested in being popular. He did not think the college should be interested in winning a popularity contest either. He thought that many colleges were more interested in increasing their enrollments and did so by lowering their standards. Hill told the Board of Trustees in 1855 that "thousands of conceited ignoramuses are spawned forth with not enough algebra to equate their minds with zero" and that "blockheads bear away the title of Bachelor of Arts; though the only art they acquired in College was the art of yelling, ringing of bells, and blowing horns in nocturnal rows."

Hill always spoke his mind and was very direct. He took aim at the president of the college, saying that "the character of the college depends mainly upon the character of its President." The president of Davidson College soon resigned in disgrace.

In 1858 Hill was offered the post of superintendent of the North Carolina Military Institute in Charlotte. He maintained this position until the outbreak of the Civil War.

As a colonel, he won distinction by winning the battle of Big Bethel near Fort Monroe, Virginia. He was promoted to brigadier general soon afterward. He participated in the battles of Seven Pines, Seven Days and Antietam. However, after the battle of Fredericksburg, his quarrelsome and opinionated nature got him into trouble. He was openly critical of his commander, General Robert E. Lee. Being a thorn in Lee's side, he was sent home to help recruit more men. In 1863 he was assigned to the Army of Tennessee and commanded one of Braxton Bragg's corps. He was involved in the battle of Chickamauga. After the battle, Hill and other generals openly criticized Bragg. Confederate President Jefferson Davis sided in favor of Bragg. The army was reorganized and Hill was left without a command. For the rest of the war he served only in small actions away from the main armies.

After the war, Hill edited a magazine in Charlotte, *The Land We Love*. He also was a popular speaker at veterans' reunions on his favorite topic, the Old South. In 1877, he became president of the University of Arkansas.

Middle Georgia Military and Agricultural College opened in Milledgeville in 1879. One of the first professors was the general's son, D.H. Hill, Jr. In 1885 at the age of sixty-four, General Hill became the president of MGM&AC. He and his wife lived in an apartment in the south wing of the Old State House. While here he strived for an improvement in the quality of the academics as well as the discipline of the students. Despite his failing health, which had bothered him for several years, he never missed a class. His medical problems were catching up to him, however.

On July 29, 1889, he resigned, writing, "There seems to be no probability that I will be able to resume my former duties. I am much feebler than I was at commencement. It is not with me a question of health and sickness but of life and death." He was suffering from stomach cancer.

He died on September 24 in Charlotte. After a funeral service at the Presbyterian church, he was buried in Davidson, North Carolina.

XVI

Dr. Lyell's Big Gully

Hidden in the woods to the southwest of the intersection of Allen Memorial Drive and Highway 49, a few miles west of Milledgeville, is a geological curiosity. It is known variously as the Big Gully, Lyell's Gully or Lyell's Big Gully. If one were to strip away the trees so the chasm could be examined clearly from the air, it would appear to be somewhat similar to a miniature Grand Canyon, except that no river flows through it.

For most people, the origins of the Gully are lost in the very distant past. One popular opinion is that the Gully is the remains of a former bed of the Oconee River that changed its course eons ago.

In 1846 famed British geologist Sir Charles Lyell was touring North America. He came to Milledgeville, which he described as "a mere village," and was shown the local geologic features by the Georgia state geologist, John Ruggles Cotting. In 1843 Cotting had written, "The worn out fields, the gullied hills and barren wastes in every part of the State…are sad mementoes of the effect of ignorance and prejudice on the part of our predecessors." One of the features that Lyell was interested in seeing was the Big Gully.

The chasm, in January 1846, was "no less than 55 feet in depth, 900 feet in length, and varying in width from 20 to 180 feet." The Gully was clearly growing in size, as Sir Charles noted that the road to Macon (now Highway 49, also called Lower Macon Road) had changed course several times as the Gully got larger and cut through the road.

The origin of the Big Gully was not in the distant geologic past. It had nothing to do with the Oconee River. What actually happened was that in the first quarter of the nineteenth century the land in Baldwin County was stripped of its forest cover for the first time ever. Rains simply eroded the soil, leaving the Big Gully. The Gully, when Lyell inspected it in 1846, was less than twenty years old.

On January 22, 1898, Dr. Harris Chappell and Dr. Luther Beeson examined the Big Gully and found it to be approximately the same size as it had been in 1846. They noted that it was "in some places covered with a thick forest growth, mainly pine trees, some of them fifty or sixty years old."

The Gully is located on land that had belonged to the Revolutionary War veteran Samuel Beckcom (also spelled Beckham). He died in November 1825. Therefore, it was probably either he himself or a descendant who cleared the land, opening it up for erosion, thus becoming the creator of the Gully. Rightly it should be called Beckcom's Gully.

Beckcom was buried in a small family cemetery that is now on the rim of the Gully. In 1909, the Daughters of the American Revolution (DAR) thought that the grave of the old soldier would be swallowed up by the Gully and decided to move his grave to Memory Hill Cemetery. For some reason they gave up the plan. However, the idea was revived by the tenacious ladies of the DAR eighty years later, and in 1991 the remains of Samuel Beckcom, but not the others in the cemetery, were moved to Memory Hill Cemetery. The DAR placed a granite marker at the original burial site, indicating that Beckcom's remains had been moved.

The old cemetery still is on the edge of the Gully and is likely to remain there, as the Gully does not appear to be advancing. As long as the trees and brush are there, the Big Gully will likely remain much as it was when it was first inspected by Sir Charles Lyell in 1846.

XVII

The Cold Water Cure

In the little mountain town of Grafenberg, Austria, in the early 1800s a young man named Vincent Priessnitz watched, fascinated, as a crippled deer healed its injured leg by holding it daily in the cold water of a mountain spring. At the age of sixteen, Priessnitz was run over by an ox cart. The surgeon said that his broken ribs would not heal. Priessnitz drank a great deal of cold mountain spring water and wrapped himself with bandages soaked in cold water. His injuries healed.

Encouraged by his success, Priessnitz treated neighbors and news of his cold water treatments soon spread. Patients started coming to him from all over Europe. He developed a series of treatments, all of which involved cold water. His treatments were all natural. Exercise, fresh air and wholesome food combined to cure his patients without the use of drugs. Establishments using his methods sprung up across Europe by the 1830s, and he became known as the father of hydrotherapy.

Milledgeville, always on the cutting edge, welcomed a similar treatment facility in February of 1846. A gentleman named T. Carlton Coyle, MD, built a facility "at the edge of town…for the reception of a small number of patients with a plunge bath for Ladies, and another for Gentlemen." Dr. Coyle selected Milledgeville because of the "gushing springs of pure fresh water." He claimed that the water was the "purest I could find among hundreds of springs I have visited and tested, from Virginia, through North and South Carolina."

He described the treatment generally as beginning "at an early hour in the morning" when a patient would be wrapped with a sheet that had been soaked in cold water. The patient was then placed on a couch, wrapped in several thick woolen blankets until only the face and head were exposed. The face was bathed with cold water. "Soon the vital warmth streams out from the patient, in a little time perspiration flows most freely from every pore…cold compresses are renewed on the head every few minutes, doors and windows are flung open in order to promote the flow of perspiration, and produce free respiration." When it was determined that the patient had perspired enough he was dropped into a cold bath that was described as "most grateful and refreshing." The idea is that "the inherent power of the constitution thus aroused for so beneficial a purpose, flings its diseases from a more, to a less diseased organ, and by degrees rids itself of all disease."

After four or five minutes in the bath, the patient was then removed and rubbed dry. He then, after some exercise, was allowed to go to breakfast. Breakfast consisted of cold water, milk and bread. Sometimes, if he was lucky, he would be able to have some fruit. After breakfast the patient then took a brisk walk, inhaling pure air. The wrapping and then dunking in the cold bath was repeated before dinner.

Dr. Coyle assured potential patients that this procedure was beneficial in "reestablishing the vital energy, and by infusing new life into the paralyzed functions of the organs." The list of diseases said to be cured by the cold water treatment was long. It included measles, small pox, brain fever, lung fevers, croup, influenza, coughs of long standing, bronchitis, gout, rheumatism, scrofula, burns, ulcers, cancer and even gunshot wounds.

Regrettably, the cold water establishment of Dr. Coyle is no longer with us. However, the treatment facility of Vincent Priessnitz survives in Austria.

XVIII

"Insane" Actor Murders: Was He Performing?

One of Atlanta's greatest amateur actors in the mid-1850s was William A. Choice. He was well known for his portrayals of the "heavy" in plays, where often his character was called upon to kill on the stage. One morning on the streets of Atlanta, he killed for real.

Bill Choice is described as being tall and fair-haired with a massive yet sinewy frame. His face, "reddened by debauchery," had blue eyes that would blaze and melt in turn. His voice was deep, rich and melodious.

Much taken with drink, he was well known—and a good customer—at many bars. On the evening of December 30, 1858, as he bellied up to the bar of the old Atlanta Hotel, he was approached by Calvin Webb, a bailiff. The bailiff showed Choice a writ against him for ten dollars. "I cannot pay it," said Choice. The bailiff replied that Choice would have to post bond.

At this moment a prominent attorney by the name of Luther J. Glenn was passing by. Choice called out to him and asked if Glenn would post security for him. Glenn replied that he would. Glenn then spoke to Webb and told the bailiff that he personally would see that the ten-dollar debt would be paid. Webb, with emphasis on "you," remarked, "If *you* say so Mr. Glenn, it is satisfactory." Choice was humiliated.

Choice invited Glenn to drink with him, but Glenn declined. Choice then turned to the bailiff and asked if he would drink with him. Webb replied, "No." Humiliated again, Choice exploded with a string of oaths and grabbed a decanter from the bar with the clear design of hitting Webb with it. The barkeeper and Glenn physically restrained Choice. They motioned Webb to leave but instead Webb pulled his revolver, ready to defend himself.

Glenn manhandled Choice into a side room and explained to him that he was in the wrong and should apologize to Webb. Choice reluctantly agreed. When they went back to the barroom, Webb was gone. Glenn, seeing that Choice was calm, went on his way. Choice stayed and drank. He drank a lot.

Late that night in a state of "beastly intoxication" according to the newspaper accounts, Choice staggered to his room in the Atlanta Hotel. Hotel guests nearby could hear him in the night talking to himself. The name "Webb" and the words "low bred scoundrel" and "insult me" were heard.

The next morning Choice went into the barroom of the Atlanta Hotel for a drink. He then drifted out for breakfast and went to another bar. Later, he wandered back to the Atlanta Hotel bar to drink some more. About ten o'clock in the morning Choice left the bar and walked the streets. It was raining. Carrying an umbrella, he had his head bent low.

He was walking on the east side of North Pryor Street when something caught his eye on the other side of the street. It was Calvin Webb, the bailiff. At a distance of forty feet, Choice pulled out a large revolver and fired at the unsuspecting Webb. He missed. Choice placed the revolver on his knee and quickly cocked it for a second shot. Webb shouted, "Don't shoot!" Choice took deliberate aim and fired, yelling, "God damn you, I will kill you anyhow." The bullet struck Webb in the right breast, killing him within seconds.

Shouting, "Damn you, take that!" Choice waved the smoking revolver over his head. He then ran down the street still waving the revolver over his head. He turned a few corners and hid himself in an abandoned building.

A mob of three thousand people assembled within minutes and began searching for the killer. Some of the men had ropes. There were cries of "Hang the damned murderer!" "Lynch him!" and "Let's get him!"

While the mob swarmed the streets, a cool headed marshal, E.T. Hunnicutt, was also searching for Choice. He soon found Choice cowering in the abandoned building. With Choice disarmed, the problem now was how to get Choice to a place of safety before the mob got him. Taking side roads Hunnicutt managed to get Choice to the jail, but the mob soon learned that Choice was in the jail and surrounded it. The angry crowd was calling for Choice. Clearly, a lynching was about to take place and there was nothing that Hunnicutt could do to prevent it.

At that moment the mayor of Atlanta, James M. Calhoun, appeared on the scene. He leaped atop a barrel and called to the irate men, "Fellow citizens! I move that we adjourn to the courthouse and discuss this matter like men. We can then decide upon a line of action, and whatever that may be, I promise to do my part in carrying it out." As if by magic, the mob settled down. They marched off to the courthouse a quarter of a mile away to discuss what should be done. Cooler heads prevailed at the courthouse and it was decided to let the law handle the situation.

The following day Choice was visited in jail by the man who was to conduct the funeral for Webb, Reverend Thomas M.W. Wilkes. Choice told him that he had killed Webb because of the influence of liquor—that when drinking he was a "mad man" and not "in my right mind." He begged the minister to tell young people of the ruin he had made of his life and to urge them to save themselves from a similar fate by keeping away from drinking, billiard tables and grog shops.

That evening, wearing a veiled costume, Choice was taken from the jail and taken to Milledgeville's jail where it was thought he would be safe from lynch mobs. He remained in Milledgeville until April, when he was indicted by the Fulton County Superior Court. His trial was set for October.

Choice assembled a fine legal team, led by Benjamin H. Hill. As there was no question that Choice was guilty of killing Webb, the defense decided to plead insanity. At trial it was brought out that Choice had been involved in a buggy accident in which he had sustained a deep gash in his head, which was claimed to have affected his brain. It was maintained that the head wound caused him to become insane when he drank and therefore he was not responsible for his actions. Further, it was asserted that he was compelled to drink to excess due to the peculiarity of the brain damage. A number of witnesses testified that Choice was insane. One cannot help but wonder if the witnesses were fooled by an actor giving the performance of a lifetime.

The jury was out for two hours and returned a verdict of guilty. Choice was sentenced to hang. His attorneys immediately made a motion for a new trial, which was denied. The case was taken to the state supreme court, which affirmed the lower court decision. William Choice was doomed. It seemed as if nothing would keep him from being executed.

There was one slim hope left, but it was so faint as to be almost an impossibility. The Georgia State legislature could be petitioned to pass a bill of pardon for William Choice. Of course, once such a bill was passed, if it could be passed, it would need to be signed by Governor Joseph E. Brown.

Defense attorney Ben Hill, for whom Ben Hill County is named, was a brilliant speaker and a fine lawyer. He was also a politician. He had run against Brown for the governorship a year earlier and was defeated. Governor Brown was not likely to do anything that would enhance the reputation of his rival.

Undeterred, Ben Hill argued the case before the legislature in Milledgeville, then the capital of Georgia. By a relatively slim margin the bill pardoning Choice was passed. However, Governor Brown refused to sign it. A second time the bill was introduced and more witnesses were brought forth to state that Choice was insane. Ben Hill stepped forward in desperation, and brought all his enormous talents to bear. The goal was to obtain two-thirds majority and thus override Governor Brown's veto. Failure would mean Choice would hang.

Before a chamber packed with legislators, curious visitors and local businessmen, Ben Hill began to speak. Choice's mother was seated in front of the president's desk. With her was Choice's sister, the wife of a prominent senator. The aged black nurse who had cared for Choice as an infant sat there, too. The three were dressed in deep mourning.

Hill hammered at two points. One was that Choice did not get a fair trial in Atlanta, as the city was inflamed against him due to the nature of the crime. He also repeatedly mentioned alleged proofs of Choice's insanity. He pointed out that in a recent case in New Jersey a woman, acting in a very sane manner, had killed her children. The woman was placed in an asylum rather than executed. Was it right to execute Choice when there was doubt of his sanity?

The powerful speaker played every emotional heartstring he could reach. After two hours the legislature adjourned for the afternoon. The following morning Hill spoke for another hour and a half. When he concluded many legislators left the chamber not wanting to cast a vote. Most of those favoring the pardon remained and thus a two-thirds majority was obtained. The veto of Governor Brown had been overridden. William Choice was spared the gallows but he was confined to the asylum in Milledgeville.

It was December 1860 and national events were moving fast. In January 1861 Georgia voted for Secession and removed itself from the Union. Within a few months the Civil War had begun.

Choice had the unusual position in the asylum of being a "day patient." One wonders where he spent his nights. Clearly, he was not considered dangerous. Whether spurred on by an urge for freedom or by patriotic feelings Choice escaped from the asylum and enlisted in Company A, Eighth Georgia Volunteer Infantry, the Rome Light Guards. He became a private on July 13, 1861, and appointed clerk at Division Headquarters. At the war's end he surrendered at Appomattox on April 9, 1865.

In the mid-1870s, Choice was returned to the asylum with severe drinking problems. He died there August 15, 1879, at the age of fifty and was buried in Milledgeville's Memory Hill Cemetery. The question will always remain: was he insane or did he cheat the hangman through a combination of a very clever defense attorney and the best performance of his life?

XIX

The Perils of Purloined Firewood

A cold winter night in the year 1866 was shattered by the sound and concussion of an explosion. The little town of Lexington, in the mountains of western Virginia, was normally a quiet and peaceful place. For the most part, the students at Virginia Military Institute and those at Washington College were a peaceful lot. The occasional rowdy drunk or ice skating party were the main exceptions.

It was a time when students respected their elders, especially when an elder happened to be a professor or member of the administration. The respect turned to awe and reverence for the president of Washington College, the honored General Robert E. Lee. A word, or even a look, from the president could shame even the most wayward student. Lee made it his business to know every student by name and every student felt the greatest obligation to make certain that he would never disappoint General Lee.

The explosion that caused the furor in 1866 occurred in the stove of one of the professors. The room was set on fire but was quickly extinguished. The professor was furious and felt certain that the bomb was maliciously planted in his stove.

The next morning President Lee discussed the explosion at chapel. He asked that anyone who had knowledge of the event would please call on him in his office. It was not long before a student stood shaking with fear in front of President Lee's desk. President Lee quietly asked for an explanation. The student said that the pile of wood for the stove in his room would diminish faster than the student was using it. Clearly, someone was helping himself at the student's woodpile. He tried to catch the thief but had not been able to do so. He then decided he would set a trap. He explained to President Lee that he had loaded a piece of firewood with gunpowder and left it in his woodpile, hoping the thief would take it.

He ended the story by saying that he did not know that the wood was being taken by a professor. Lee laughed and told the student that his plan was a good one but that his powder charge was too heavy—next time, use less powder. He then dismissed the very relieved student.

Thirteen years later, a similar event took place in Milledgeville. Charles Bonner was frustrated by someone taking wood from his woodpile. He tried to identify the firewood thief but was never able to catch the person. Like the student, he loaded a stick of wood with gunpowder. His aggravation was evident when he used a full pound of powder. It was a fearsome bomb.

At 8:00 a.m. on Saturday, November 8, 1879, Milledgeville was rocked by a terrific blast. No lives were lost. However, the home where the stove was located was badly damaged and on fire. The fire was soon extinguished and the firewood thief, who lived behind Bonner's store, was identified.

In reporting the incident the newspaper sagely commented, "People who steal firewood would do well hereafter to burn it out doors." I like to think that General Lee would have laughed and heartily approved of the sentiment.

XX

HONOR RESTORED THROUGH BLOODSHED

Hancock street in downtown Milledgeville was the scene of a hailstorm of bullets Saturday afternoon, November 19, 1898, which left one man dead on the sidewalk and five others wounded. The cause of the gunfight was minor in itself, but injured pride was involved and would not be satisfied without confrontation, shooting and bloodshed.

The trouble began about noon at the restaurant of eighteen-year-old Thomas Finney. Bill Stanley, thirty, accompanied by his twenty-four-year-old brother Julian, was not satisfied with his food. They had eaten soup, broiled steak, pork, sausage and coffee as well as light bread and biscuit. After eating the meal, Bill Stanley said he had been served only half a dinner. Thomas Finney told Bill Stanley that he had been served what he had ordered. Bill Stanley responded that it was a "damned lie." Young Thomas Finney tried to explain and offered to give the Stanleys anything else they wanted when Bill Stanley called him a son of a bitch and slapped his face. The Stanleys then left the restaurant.

Thomas Finney, angry and humiliated, put a .32-caliber Iver-Johnson pistol in his pocket, saying, "If he slaps me again I will kill him," and went across the street to the wheelwright shop of his father, W.O. "Bill" Finney. Upon hearing the story Bill Finney went out onto Wayne Street and located Police Officer Lawrence who he brought back to the restaurant so his son could repeat the story to him. Bill Finney demanded the arrest of Bill Stanley.

Bill Stanley was arrested and posted bond for his appearance before the mayor on Monday morning. Police Officer Lawrence reported to Bill Finney that he had arrested Bill Stanley in hopes that it would calm the Finneys' hot temper. But an arrest was not good enough. Saying that Bill Stanley "had cursed his son and [Stanley] had to apologize or one of them would have to die," Bill Finney was as angry as ever. Lawrence told him to go back to his business. But that was not to be. Once set in motion the need for satisfaction was not easily restrained.

The Finneys walked up and down crowded Hancock Street looking for the Stanleys for restoration of their honor and for trouble. In front of the store of L.H. Thomas, just west of the intersection of Hancock and Wayne Streets, they came face to face with Bill and Julian Stanley. Bill Finney walked up to Bill Stanley and said, "You called my boy a son of a bitch!" and shot him once in the chest with a .38 Iver-Johnson revolver. Bill Stanley grabbed Finney's arm while pulling his own revolver, a .38 Smith & Wesson, and fired six shots at Bill Finney. Thomas Finney immediately fired four shots from his .32 Iver-Johnson at the Stanleys. His fire was met by only one shot from Julian Stanley's .32 Smith & Wesson.

Police Officers Lawrence and Terry were immediately on the scene. They found Bill Finney dying on the sidewalk. Bill Stanley came out of a store with his empty pistol still in his hand. Julian Stanley was inside the store bleeding from a wound to his face. Thomas Finney was shot in the leg and side. Two stray bullets had struck an unnamed black man and a black woman, inflicting minor wounds.

The body of Bill Finney was taken to his home on South Wayne Street. Thomas Finney was taken to Carrington's Drug Store on the southwest corner of Wayne and Hancock Streets, where his wounds were treated. The Stanleys were initially treated at the store of L.H. Thomas on Hancock Street and later were taken to the Harper House Hotel where they remained for several days recovering from their wounds.

The following day, Sunday, the coroner's jury investigated the shootings. After hearing the evidence, they brought the following verdict: "That W.O. 'Bill' Finney came to his death from pistol wounds inflicted by W.B. 'Bill' Stanley; and that Stanley killed said Finney in self defense."

Bill Stanley's chest wound healed but the bullet was never located and never extracted. He survived a bout of typhoid fever during the summer of 1899 but died of blood poisoning as a result of the bullet on January 2, 1900. He is buried at Salem Baptist Church.

Bill Finney is buried in Milledgeville's Memory Hill Cemetery. He is in east side, section A, lot 18, grave number 1. A few graves away, in the same lot, is his son Thomas, who died October 14, 1961, almost sixty-three years after the shooting.

Julian Stanley is also buried in Memory Hill Cemetery. He died on April 20, 1952. He is in east side, section D, lot 85, grave number 1. The grave of Julian Stanley is within sight of the graves of the Finneys.

The disagreement over a lunch and misplaced honor had cost two men their lives and two others serious injuries, plus wounding two innocent bystanders. The families, both highly respectable, lived with the consequences of that fateful day for over sixty years until the last of the participants found the peace of the grave.

XXI

Moonshine and Murder

Taxing liquor and the violence that accompanies it is nothing new. The liquor tax was common in the colonial era, and in 1794 the Whiskey Rebellion in western Pennsylvania was a reaction to the tax by the citizenry.

Historically, Georgians have distilled peaches, corn and apples into brandy and whiskey as a way to raise cash and dispose of excess farm produce. Today we think of moonshine as a mountain activity, but it was a widespread practice carried out by farmers all across the state. Distilling was thought by many to be a harmless enterprise.

During the Civil War, the U.S. government established the Internal Revenue Service, which collected taxes on items considered luxuries such as tobacco and liquor. After the war, the private distillers of liquor continued making the product and were very frequently reluctant to pay any taxes. In the South, devastated by war, distillers faced economic hard times and sought some relief through what they considered their right to produce through their own labor. This brought them into conflict with the revenuers, the federal agents charged with enforcing the tax laws. The conflict became a war of sorts.

The moonshiners frequently would engage in gunfights with the revenuers. They would also intimidate the nearby population to keep them from providing any helpful information to the revenuers. The residents also would often take the side of the moonshiners in court cases. Many of the residents, even those without family ties, felt a kinship with their moonshiner neighbors. The federal government was often seen as an outsider attempting to impose taxes and behavior standards on the countryman.

One such incident resulting in a shooting took place September 10, 1878, in Hancock County when revenue agents attempted to arrest twenty-five-year-old Pleasant T. "Doshe" Ennis and his twenty-eight-year-old brother Erasmus A. "Ras" Ennis. There are two versions of the encounter. The lawmen have their version and the Ennis side of the story comes from letters written by P.T. Ennis to the *Union Recorder* newspaper. The newspaper went out of its way to give both sides to the story. The paper referred to the Ennis brothers as belonging to a "large and respectable family" and reported that they "have been peaceable law-abiding citizens, and this trouble has been precipitated by a set of unfortunate circumstances and bad management." The paper reported, "Our citizens were greatly surprised and shocked at the result of the unfortunate expedition [during which the shooting occurred]. That there is much sympathy for the Ennises is not denied, but that there is any disposition to uphold them, or any man, or set of men, in the violation of law, is a slander upon a peace-loving community."

According to the lawmen, Deputy U.S. Marshal B.D. Lumsden and his deputies Jack Kimbrew, James Laney and James Moore went to the Ennis place in western Hancock County with the intent to arrest P.T. Ennis and E.A. Ennis for illicit distilling. According to the official report, Lumsden was cautioned that the Ennis brothers had "threatened violence should any attempt be made to arrest" them. The lawmen arrived shortly after dark hoping to find both men at home. Marshal Lumsden hailed the Ennis house and a black man came outside. Lumsden asked if Mr. Ennis was at home. The man replied that he was. Lumsden and Kimbrew followed the man to the house. A white man appeared at the door. Kimbrew asked, "Is this Mr. Ennis?" The report described what happened next: "Before anything more was said, a shot was fired from inside the door, the charge taking effect in Kimbrew's arm and nearly severing it at the elbow. Deputy Lumsden then drew his pistol and fired one shot at the party in the door who had discharged the gun.

Another of the defendants appearing, and the firing at the officers being continued, Laney, who was coming to their rescue, was shot down. Lumsden's pistol refusing to work, he was obliged to retreat with his wounded comrades." Laney was struck in the thigh and abdomen by small shot from a shotgun. The wounded men were taken to the McComb Hotel on the southwest corner of Wayne and Greene Streets in Milledgeville. They were attended by Drs. Hall, Harris and Whitaker. Kimbrew died early the following day. Laney recovered.

Doshe Ennis sent a letter to the *Union Recorder* dated September 11 describing the incident. According to Ennis:

> *About dark, a party of men came to my gate and hailed. Chapell Russell, a darkie in my employment went to the gate to see who it was. Myself and family, together with my brother and Miss Zillfair Blizzard, were sitting at the table in the kitchen eating supper. The men asked, "did Mr. Ennis live there?" and Chapell answered that he did. They then said, "Tell Mr. Ennis to come out," as they wanted to see him. The servant came back at once followed by two or three men and told me there were some gentlemen there who wanted to see me. I put my little girl down off my lap and stepping to the door one of the men asked if that was Mr. Ennis. I replied that it was, and he immediately drew his pistol and fired at my head, the powder burning my face and eyes. In the mean time I and my brother picked up our guns and fired at him before he could repeat his shot. They ran around the kitchen and it being a log house without the cracks being stopped, one or two of them halted and fired at me through the cracks. We then went into the yard and continued firing on them till they were out of sight. We fired seven times in all, using two double-barreled guns and firing three times with a pistol. I and my brother then quit the yard and reloading our guns could have killed the party, but would not use the advantage we had of them as it never has been our intention to hurt any body, but rather to keep out of the way.*

In another letter, dated September 13, signed by both Doshe Ennis and his brother Ras Ennis, more information from the Ennis point of view is provided. Referring to comments made in print by Officer Laney, the Ennises wrote:

> *Mr. Laney says that "Kimbrew and Lumsden went to the front door of the house and hailed and that one of the Ennis' came out, he did not hear what was said, Ennis then walked to one side of the house where the kitchen joined it." Now to show that Laney lied, the kitchen is all of 15 or 20 feet from the house. You will find in the statement of P.T. Ennis, sent you a few days since, a true statement of the matter in regard to who went to the gate when they hailed and what words were passed before the firing took place and who shot first. We wished to show to you and to the people of Georgia, what was the cause of this whole difficulty: I, P.T. Ennis, ran a still for Mr. W.E. Haygood, last year, the same being registered in Mr. Haygood's name and belonging to him. We agreed to go halves—making only sixty gallons of brandy in all. I took the brandy in my charge—made the returns in Haygood's name as he could not attend to it at that time. W.J. White, Deputy U.S. Collector for 3rd District, wrote for a guager and none came. I wrote and Mr. Wilson also wrote for one and none came. I waited until in December, when I sold forty gallons of the brandy to one Jule* [Julian] *Cumming and this brings my brother E.A. Ennis into the transaction, and all that he ever did in the whole affair was to bring an order from me to Cumming for the money for the brandy. This I will swear to as he had nothing else whatever to do with it. We have offered to pay the taxes and guaging since that, but they told us we would have to stand a trial. We refused to do this as it was their fault and not ours all the while that the brandy was not guaged and stamped. We ask you now as men of Georgia, to make a self case of it. Who is right and who is wrong? All we can now say is that "God will give justice to all."*

The case becomes more complicated at this point. The Ennises referred to Jule Cumming. On May 5, Cumming had been crossing Wayne Street in Milledgeville about 9:00 p.m. when he was shot three times by an unknown assailant. Cumming made an affidavit that he had been shot by P.T. Ennis. Immediately, C.W. Ennis, a third brother, put a notice in the *Union Recorder* saying he could prove that P.T. Ennis was twelve miles away when the shooting occurred. Apparently in retaliation, P.T. Ennis's home was destroyed in an arson fire on May 7.

On May 7, the *Union Recorder* commented, "Mr. [P.T.] Ennis has always borne the character of a good, quiet citizen, and we believe it is the general opinion of the community that, however ready he might be to meet an antagonist in an open field, he is not the man to be guilty of a sneaking, cowardly assassination."

The last week of May, Doshe Ennis and Ras Ennis were arrested, along with several others, for conspiracy to murder Jule Cumming. They and their attorneys went to Savannah for a hearing. The charge was amended to conspiracy to intimidate a witness. It seems that Cumming had given evidence to the revenue department and it was thought that the attempt on his life was done to prevent his testifying. The defense attorneys filed a motion for dismissal saying that there was no case currently before the United States Courts where Cumming was a witness. Since he was not a witness, the charge could not be sustained and the case was dismissed.

Perhaps in an effort to divert suspicion or muddy the waters, one of the men arrested along with the Ennises claimed that the real shooter of Cumming was one John T. Arnold, the son of the Milledgeville Sheriff Obadiah Arnold. The accusation was vehemently denied by the sheriff.

The inquest held after the September tenth shooting at the Ennis place returned the verdict that Kimbrew "came to his death by a gunshot wound delivered by a white man standing in the door of P.T. Ennis' house."

Marshal Lumsden reported the shooting to his superiors in Atlanta. Captain John W. Anderson was dispatched to Milledgeville to take over the case. On the fourteenth, Anderson led a posse of thirty "of the best citizens of Milledgeville" to capture the Ennis brothers. Among the posse were Judge D.B. Sanford, Judge F.G. Dubignon, Sheriffs O. Arnold and Edwards, County Treasurer Thomas, Scott (the coroner), U.S. Marshal Lamar and Drs. Shinholster and Harris.

The posse surrounded the residence of the Ennis brothers but found no one home. They searched large parts of Hancock and Baldwin Counties without success. Nearby residents advised that the brothers had left the area and probably gone to Texas. Captain Anderson reported the situation to his superior, Colonel O.P. Fitzsimons, the U.S. Marshal for Georgia.

The Ennis brothers were not to be found. Colonel Fitzsimons commented, "It is strange that the Ennis brothers, who claim to be so innocent, and to have been so ruthlessly assailed in their own home should fail to give themselves up to the authorities."

The October 23 *Augusta Chronicle* carried news of the Hancock County Superior Court. The grand jury

> brought a true bill [indictment] *against the revenue officers who attempted to kill the "Ennis boys" some time ago. It can be proven, it is said, that the officers were drunk—that they fired upon Ennis before explaining their business—that the Ennises did not resist until fired at, and that they acted in self-defense. One of the officers was killed and another wounded. Warrants for the arrest of the revenue officials will be immediately placed in the hands of the proper officers, and a test question made whether or not these select Federal parties can ride roughshod over unoffending citizens with impunity. All good citizens pronounce the affair an outrage on Georgians and are rightly indignant.*

The moonshine war between the revenue officers and the Ennises did not involve further gunplay. The courts took up the fights. Charges and counter charges were filed in this and many other moonshine cases. It has been estimated that four-fifths of all federal law-enforcement efforts and court cases in Georgia involved illegal liquor sales. The court system and the federal agencies were bogged down by these legal actions. The moonshiners continued their clandestine activities for generations.

The Ennises did not go to Texas. According to family tradition, they hid out in the swamps to avoid capture. Doshe's wife and her sister (who would later marry Ras) are said to have brought food to their hiding places. The men were never brought to trial and eventually came out of hiding and lived life once again among their neighbors.

Ras Ennis died in 1926. He was a longtime Sunday school superintendent. His brother Doshe died in 1891 from pneumonia.

He was a farmer and also tax receiver for the county. C.W. Ennis was elected sheriff in January of 1879, a position he effectively and honestly served for over twenty years.

XXII

Mary Mapp's Revolutionary Dough Raiser

I KNOW NOTHING OF BAKING bread. I am informed, however, that it is necessary for the dough to rise before it is put into the oven to be baked. Heat is required to get the dough to rise but not so much heat that the dough begins to bake.

Therein lies the rub. How does one warm the dough without getting it too warm? It can't be put into the oven as the oven is too hot. One might place the dough next to the oven but then the heat would be uneven. The dough could also be placed in bright sunlight. But as the process of dough rising takes many hours, using the sun could be a problem, especially on cloudy days or at night.

I have been told that modern bread bakers have a way of handling this problem. They turn on the clothes dryer and put their dough on top of the dryer. The dryer keeps the dough warm so it will rise. Obviously, this is not a solution that was available to women in the nineteenth century.

Mary E. Mapp of Milledgeville solved the problem in 1891. She submitted drawings and a detailed description of her Dough Raiser device to the U.S. Patent Office in November of 1891, and on January 26, 1896, she was granted patent number 467,820.

Mary Mapp's device had four wooden legs and stood about three feet tall. There was an airtight upper chamber, called the dough-raising chamber, made of wood. One side of the dough-raising chamber had a door with a latch. This was where the dough is placed. There was a row of small vertical perforations on one side of the chamber. A thermometer was attached over these holes on the outside so the internal temperature of the dough-raising chamber could be monitored by the baker.

Directly below the dough-raising chamber was the heart of the device. This was the heat distributor. It was a sheet metal airtight box that had the same dimensions as the floor of the upper chamber. The heat distributor was about one inch thick and was placed directly below the upper chamber.

Below the heat distributor was an open space tall enough for two kerosene lamps to be placed so that the tops of their chimneys were just below the bottom of the heat distributor.

The heat from the lamps would heat the heat distributor by convection. The heat passed through the heat distributor to the upper surface of the bottom of the dough-raising chamber by conduction, and the dough-raising chamber was heated secondarily by radiation from the entire surface of the bottom of the dough-raising chamber.

This clever device had two main points that separated it from any other Dough Raiser available at that time. First, the dough-raising chamber was uniformly heated from the bottom. In addition, a further advantage of the device was that the gases from the burning oil in the lamps were kept away from the dough-raising chamber so the dough would not be contaminated with fumes that would impair the taste of the bread, as occurred in other dough-raising devices.

Mary Mapp, the unsung inventor of Milledgeville, deserves her place in our history. As far as I know, she was the only female inventor in Baldwin County during the nineteenth century. I am not aware that an example of Mary Mapp's Dough Raiser is still in existence. I like to think, however, that every woman in Milledgeville rushed out to purchase the device and consequently made better bread.

XXIII

Let There Be Light

It's not news to anyone that we take the electric light for granted. However, during the winter of 2005 when most Milledgeville residents lost their power due to an ice storm, some for an extended period of time, we were forcefully reminded what it is like not to have the ability to just throw a switch and have light in our homes.

Little more than 125 years ago no one in Milledgeville had ever seen an electric light. On November 14, 1879, their world was changed. The electric light came to Milledgeville—not as a utility for each consumer but rather as a show in a circus.

It's hard to overexaggerate the enthusiasm and anticipation surrounding this event. For weeks Cole's New York and New Orleans Circus had been advertised in the newspaper as well as on posters plastered on walls around town. According to the newspapers there was a "gorgeous street pageant" with "wild beasts," and something called a "great hippodramatic street pageant." The circus was so large it arrived in three separate trains.

The response from the community and for miles around was overwhelming. The newspaper gushed, "Never, not even the day [Mike] Shaw was hung, have we seen so many people in Milledgeville." The paper continued, "some estimated the number of visitors at ten thousand. There were not less than four thousand people under the canvas in the afternoon." The streets were "almost impassable—the wave of human flesh rocked restlessly like the seaweed."

But the people didn't come for the animals or the street parade. They came for three things: the tallest man and woman on earth and the electric light. To us, the tallest man and woman on earth are just tall people. However, the electric light was something very, very special.

The apparatus used was called a "Bush Electric Light," the machinery for which is driven by a thirty-horsepower engine and a twenty-horsepower boiler, as well as twenty thousand yards of insulated telegraph wire. This was not an incandescent light like a modern light bulb but rather an arc light.

The *Union Recorder* described the light as "a great, bright, dazzling light, yet it emits no heat. A newspaper of the finest print can be read two miles [away]." It was "dazzling and brilliant light, so far surpassing all other illuminations that the darkest night is penetrated for miles with its fiery darts, and the smallest objects are distinctly discernable. The light being a pure white and nearly a perfect imitation of the most brilliant sunshine, its effect on the vast audience present was very pleasing." Nothing had ever been seen like it in Milledgeville. "A thousand gas jets has the appearance of a few tallow candles when placed by the side of this wonderful electric light."

The crowd was amazed and delighted. The fifty-cent admission (children twenty-five cents) was a pittance that allowed them to see the future. The light was said to be the "greatest discovery of the present century" and "Heaven's own gift to man."

It would be another ten years before the electric light was common in Milledgeville homes. But residents never forgot the evening they saw that first electric light turn night into day.

XXIV

THE SACKING OF WESTOVER PLANTATION

During the fall of 1864, the last year of the Civil War, Union General William Tecumseh Sherman conducted an operation now known as the "March to the Sea." After his victory at the battle of Atlanta, Sherman could march virtually unopposed anywhere throughout the South.

Cutting off his communication with the North, Sherman marched from Atlanta to Savannah—the Sea. Despite his huge train of supply wagons, it was not possible to bring along provisions for his sixty-thousand-man army. To some extent the army would have to live off the land by taking what it needed. In addition, Sherman wanted the presence of his army marching through the South—endangering life and property—to encourage dissent and desertions from the Confederate army as the Southern soldiers feared for their families at home.

Since the war, the story of the march has been told and retold. It has become a tale of Sherman cutting a path of utter destruction ninety miles wide from Atlanta to Savannah, burning everything in his path. That description is somewhat of an exaggeration. Railroads were torn up; bridges burned; stores of cotton, food and produce of any kind were destroyed. Towns generally were spared although factories and railroad depots were usually burned.

Individual farms and plantations would usually be stripped bare of anything of value or edible. Dwellings, especially if people were present, usually were not burned. But they very often were ransacked.

One of the finest plantation houses in Georgia was located four miles northwest of Milledgeville. It had been built in the 1820s by the wealthy Benjamin S. Jordan. He will be remembered for the monument that stands over his grave in Memory Hill Cemetery. The monument is thirty feet tall with an angel on the top and is very similar to the Pulaski Monument in Savannah.

Benjamin Jordan died before the war. His son, Leonidas A. Jordan, called Lee by his friends, inherited Westover Plantation as well as several other plantations. As one of the wealthiest men in the state Lee could—and did—make his home a showplace. The only problem with the plantation was that it was located in Sherman's path.

Preceding the main body of troops were bands of foragers, known as "bummers," who would fan out for miles along the route of march. They did a lot more than forage for supplies. They were experts in finding buried or hidden valuables, making off with whatever food was available and destroying crops or farm animals that they did not take with them. They would often burn or destroy farm buildings. Countless homes were ransacked by them. Their excesses were held only loosely in check by officers.

On November 22, 1864, the bummers arrived at the elegant Westover Plantation. Officers soon appeared as Jordan's overseer, a former New Yorker named Allen, was voluntarily offering the contents of the wine cellar. In exchange for the hospitality, guards were placed around the house. It seems that Mr. Allen, in his enthusiasm, consumed a good deal of wine himself and passed out. The officers carried him off to bed. When he awoke he was probably very surprised not only to find himself in bed but also that the house was still standing and untouched.

The rank and file did not join in the wine party although they watched through the windows. As one participant commented, the men had to "confine themselves to a skirmish with the poultry and hogs around the yard, which they soon cleared out."

The magnificent home and its furnishings survived the day. But the following day, some foragers were fired upon—and some killed allegedly after surrendering—by Confederate soldiers at Westover.

Early on the morning of the twenty-fourth, Thanksgiving Day, 150 Union soldiers were sent to Westover. Believing that the enemy might still be there, the soldiers approached the house from three sides. A few Confederates fired at the advancing troops but fled after a momentary skirmish. Some were captured.

A Union soldier, Captain James Royal Ladd of the 113th Ohio Volunteers, gave a detailed account of what transpired at Westover, which he said, "proved to be one of the richest furnished things I ever saw in my life."

> *The furniture was of the most costly kind, chairs were all rosewood trimmed with satin, sofa the same. All the crockery was china of best material. All the stands and bureaus were marble top. Such was the sitting and dining rooms, but we will step into the parlor. The handsomest carpet I ever saw covered the floor. On the center table was a chandelier beautiful beyond description. The window curtains reaching from the ceiling to the floor were satin lined with straw colored silk. Two large mirrors reaching from the floor to the ceiling and everything else in keeping. All that money could purchase to make a house beautiful was there. Its rooms above were equally well furnished. The silver plate but little of it could be found, it having been removed.*

Captain Ladd also described the sacking of Westover:

> *The boys were drawn up on a line and ordered to stack arms and then to go in and clean the concern out and now a scene was enacted which beggars all description. They completely demolished everything. It looked wicked to see such splendid furniture go to pieces. The house was ransacked from cellar to garret and everything they did not want to carry away was destroyed. Crash followed crash and all the comforts and luxuries of a splendid home were soon in ruins. The garden*

was also beautiful, two large hot houses containing all kinds of choice plants and flowers were destroyed. The out buildings were in keeping. A splendid barouche carriage shared the same fate and after all this had been done the torch hid it from view. But such has been the fate of several plantations.

The main house, however, was not burned. One cannot help but wonder at the thoughts of overseer Allen as he wandered through the wreckage after the Union army had moved on.

In a few days the march continued and Sherman's army crossed the Oconee River on its way to Savannah. The populace scrambled to find food and salvage what was left of their belongings. Lee Jordan decided to sell Westover. On December 20 he placed advertisements in the Milledgeville, Macon and Augusta newspapers proclaiming:

Westover. A beautiful Residence and Plantation for Sale.
I now offer my plantation, well known as the late residence of Benjamin S. Jordan, within five miles of Milledgeville, on the Eatonton Railroad, handsomely improved, fine dwelling, with good out-houses, barns, stables, etc., for sale. In front of the dwelling there is a beautiful flower yard, handsomely ornamented, and one of the finest and best collections of plants and flowers in Middle Georgia. Also, a fine apple and peach orchard. the tract contains 850 acres of good land, about 250 in the woods. Furniture, stock, etc., can be had with the place.

Considering what we know took place, this description of Westover is certainly optimistic. Perhaps he intended on making extensive repairs prior to sale. The magnificent Westover home survived the war only to be consumed by fire in 1954.

XXV

The Worst Christmas Milledgeville Ever Had

We all like to think about the warmly remembered Christmases of the past—visions of Currier and Ives prints, maybe some snow, friends, family and the wonderful smells of Christmas dinner. Of course, not all Christmases are like that. Some are better than others, but none can compare with Christmas 1864, which was the worst Christmas those in the path of General Sherman ever had.

It should be remembered that by December 1864 the Civil War had been raging for three and a half years. Most able-bodied men were in the military. Those left behind, unless they were demonstrably decrepit or in a protected occupation, between the ages of sixteen and sixty had been called out by Governor Joseph E. Brown to defend Georgia from the enemy. Union General William T. Sherman had burned Atlanta, and in November his troops poured out on their infamous March to the Sea. Christmas was just a month away when the little city of perhaps four thousand souls was invaded by an army of thirty thousand enemy soldiers.

The *Confederate Union* newspaper of December 6, 1864, in its first issue after Sherman's troops left here, claimed,

> *Robbery of every kind, and in every degree was the order of the day. They seemed to think that every thing we had belonged to them; and that it was a very great crime to hide any thing*

from them, and hiding did very little good, for they are the most experienced and adroit thieves that we ever heard of, and know exactly where to look for hidden treasure. If there was no hell before there ought to be one purposely for Sherman and his army...The attention of the enemy was principally directed to poultry, stock, provisions of all kinds, hogs, harness, money and valuables. [Within the city] *a stillness almost Sabbath like pervades our business streets, and the blackened, sightless wall of the Penitentiary, Arsenal, Magazine and Depot remind us constantly of the presence of the vandal hordes of Sherman.*

It was a desperate and grim situation. Food was in very short supply. The newspapers published pleas to those in the country who had any food to bring it to Milledgeville, saying the situation was "a question of life and death. Sherman's army, whilst they remained with us, destroyed everything eatable." People were literally living from day to day on whatever they could scrounge. A week before Christmas, a lady described seeing "people of the neighborhood wandering over [the field where the enemy had camped] seeking for anything they could find to eat, even picking up grains of corn that were scattered around where the Yankees had fed their horses."

In today's world many often look to the federal government for help when a disaster strikes—or at least the state government. In 1864 things were different. With an enemy army parading through the Deep South, the Confederate government in Richmond, Virginia, had more pressing issues on its hands than sending relief to little Milledgeville. The State of Georgia government had fled Milledgeville with the approach of Sherman's army, so it was in no position to send aid, even if it had aid to send. Milledgeville was in a tight spot. Starvation was real.

Three weeks after Sherman left Milledgeville, James A. Seddon, the secretary of war in Richmond, sent a letter to Milledgeville Mayor Boswell B. DeGraffenried, advising him that a London merchant, Alexander Collie, had given the Confederacy a fund for charitable purposes. DeGraffenried was authorized to draw $5,000 from the fund for "the relief of those who have been reduced to poverty by the recent passage of the enemy through Georgia." DeGraffenried graciously thanked Seddon, saying that the money "could not have been bestowed on a more needy and grateful people." However, the mayor knew only too well that when rabbits were selling for $5 each, in inflated Confederate currency, $5,000 would not go far in feeding a population of four thousand.

Some felt a bitterness toward the Georgia lawmakers who were unable to provide any assistance. After reading the English statesman and political philosopher Edmund Burke's 1795 essay "Thoughts and Details on Scarcity," Seth N. Broughton, editor of the *Confederate Union*, wrote that he "concluded Burke knew more in one minute than the Georgia Legislature did in 40 days, about supply and demand."

General Howell Cobb, the commander of the Georgia troops, took matters into his own hands. He sent to Milledgeville, in government wagons, five thousand rations of meal and eighteen beefs belonging to the state government. However, these relief efforts were just a drop in the bucket. The citizenry mostly scratched out an existence on their own.

The *Confederate Union* reported that on Friday, December 23, "a scene in the streets of Milledgeville [occurred] which was so novel and interesting that we had to make a note of it. It was nothing more, nor less, than a generous hearted country gentleman dispensing from his wagon, to his friends and fellow citizens, fine, large spare-ribs, with the simple question, 'will you accept a rib?' We know that the native modesty of the man would shrink at public mention of his name. Hence we withhold it. We only wish there were more such men in the county." We, 141 years later, wish the name of this country gentleman had been made public. We can only speculate as to his identity.

Editor Broughton wrote, "Christmas has come, but it is not the Christmas of the good old days before the War. It will be a 'merry Christmas' to few, if any; and far between will be the happy social gatherings which has been so marked a feature of this joyous season... for the great number it will be a dull and dreary Christmas."

The newspaper continued the following week:

> *The past week has indeed been a gloomy one, around, above, below, inside. The news was gloomy, and the weather seemed*

to take its cue from the military situation. Eggs are rare articles about here, since Sherman's hen roost robbers paid us visit; and that cut off the supply of egg-nog, the only solace that many could have found under the many depressed surroundings. It was enough to give any good man, even the editor of a newspaper, a fit of the blues to have lived in the last week of 1864. Nobody invited us to a "merry Christmas" at their house, and we had nothing at ours to be merry with, no turkey to stop the aching in the void; no doughnuts to pacify the restless gastric juice, and no corn juice to put all the juices in us to running around and keeping warm. Oh, it was not like Christmas was in boyhood days. The gloomy weather is gone, the season of disaster to our army, we pray God is over. Let us hope for brighter and better days, and strive to be better, and we certainly will be happier men.

Brighter and better days did come, although it would be a very long time before bad memories were dimmed. Readers of the *Southern Recorder*, accustomed to reading distressing war news, no doubt welcomed an advertisement that appeared in the January 17, 1865 edition that proclaimed that a gentleman would be arriving in Milledgeville "for the purpose of tuning pianos." Clearly, Milledgeville was making a comeback. So would the other cities and towns that suffered along the path of Sherman's March to the Sea.

XXVI

Breaking the Chains of Legend

Part of the charm of Milledgeville is its wealth of colorful legends of the past. Among them are legends of General Sherman, various ghosts and church organs playing sweet music due to the molasses poured into them.

Another story has been told and retold beyond the memory of our oldest residents. It concerns the three chain links that adorn some of the graves in Memory Hill Cemetery. These links are not carved onto a tombstone but rather are actual links of chain attached to a rod at a grave site. The story, as countless trolley riders have heard, is that the three chain links indicate that a person was born a slave, lived a slave and died a slave.

Despite having been in literally hundreds of cemeteries all over the country, I had never seen the three actual chain links until coming to Memory Hill. The connection to slavery did not seem credible to me. If the story were true, there should be a huge number of graves marked with the chain links. However, I did not have an alternative theory. None of the graves marked with the chain links is identified with a name, so I did not have a person I could research for the answer. For several years, the problem of the chains remained a nagging mystery for me.

A few years ago I formulated a theory. Three chain links were the emblem of the Grand United Order of Odd Fellows. By this theory the graves were of former members of that fraternal order. I found that a lodge of the Odd Fellows did exist in Milledgeville. My investigations had not progressed beyond that point.

In March of 2006, Memory Hill Cemetery was surveyed by the Chicora Foundation of Columbia, South Carolina, which is a professional historic preservation organization. They are experts in archaeological and historical research. One of their areas of expertise is historic cemeteries. I asked the director, Dr. Michael Trinkley, what the chain links represented. Without hesitation, he replied that it indicated membership in the Odd Fellows. I asked him if he had ever seen separate chain links such as in Memory Hill in any other cemetery and he said that he had not. He suggested that the links were probably a custom of the local Odd Fellows lodge or that a local talented member made them especially for deceased members.

I am confident now that the chain links in Memory Hill are associated with membership in the Odd Fellows. However, I am also confident that the legend of the chain links and slavery will continue forever. It's far too good a story to be overshadowed by mere facts. This is, after all, Milledgeville, where the past and legends never really die.

XXVII

Milledgeville Tunnel is Found!

For generations there has been a persistent legend in Milledgeville that an ancient tunnel, predating the Civil War, exists connecting the former State House building with the Old Governor's Mansion. The belief in this tunnel is very strong and many people claim to have seen the tunnel at some time in the past. However, modern historians can find no historical evidence that the tunnel was ever constructed. The tunnel itself has never, publicly, been shown to exist. That has all changed. The Milledgeville Tunnel has been found. There is no question about it. Not only has documentation been found to show that the tunnel existed in the past, but I have actually gone through the tunnel and have a witness.

It happened in an unexpected way. I was in special collections at the GCSU library going through boxes of old letters from the Civil War. In particular, I was looking for people who had been in Milledgeville during Sherman's occupation.

I was reading a letter by a former Confederate soldier, Jonathan Caraker, dated April 1877. He described how he had been in Milledgeville on leave in November of 1864 when Sherman's forces approached Milledgeville. To my astonishment, Caraker wrote that he hid from Sherman's troops for several days inside the tunnel.

Caraker mentioned that many of Sherman's officers stayed at the Milledgeville Hotel and that he could hear them talking while he was hiding in the tunnel. Suddenly, it dawned on me. People have always thought that the long lost tunnel went from the State House to the Governor's Mansion. But it did not and does not. It went from the Milledgeville Hotel to the Governor's Mansion. The Milledgeville Hotel was located on the northeast corner of Greene and Wayne Streets and was the best hotel in Milledgeville. When the legislature was in session the Milledgeville Hotel was always full of legislators. They spent the night there, ate, drank and conducted informal business there. It would make sense that if the legislators wanted a tunnel it would go from the place where they lived rather than the place where they worked.

The new Magnolia State Bank is now on the corner where the Milledgeville Hotel used to be. The old hotel was physically larger than the current bank. The hotel occupied an area that included the building where the *Baldwin Bulletin* has its offices now. I asked Pam Beer, the editor, if I could look around in the basement. She thought I was nuts but told me to go ahead.

I rummaged around in the basement looking at the floor and walls for some sign of the tunnel. I found an area on the west wall about four feet wide and six feet tall that was cement blocks rather than stone and brick as were the other walls. I thought that was odd and asked Pam if she'd mind if I broke a small hole in the wall so I could look and see if there was anything behind it. She said she didn't care, so I took a hammer and broke a hole in the wall big enough to look in with a flashlight.

I couldn't see anything behind the wall. It was dark but obviously "nothing" was there. Instead of finding soil there was an empty space. I kept making the hole larger trying to see something. Finally, it became so large I could see a brick vaulted roof on the other side of the cement block wall. I shined the light into the distance, and as far as I could see there was just darkness. It was a tunnel with dirt floor, brick walls and vaulted brick ceiling.

Excited, I ran upstairs and told Pam she had to see this. She took one look through the hole and said I could tear the rest of the wall down. Down it came. We got another flashlight and walked into the tunnel. We were under Wayne Street. It was cold and damp. There was air blowing from the farther end. The tunnel was about six feet wide and six feet high, completely made of bricks.

Milledgeville Tunnel is Found!

This was really exciting. We slowly walked down the tunnel, shining our lights on the walls. It seemed perfectly solid and there were no places that appeared to be caving in. The tunnel slowly descended; we soon realized that we were past Century Bank and going under the parking lot on the west side of the bank. We were scared out of our wits when we heard a loud bang, a metal sound, coming from the walls of the tunnel. Pam figured it out first; it was a car going over a manhole cover on Greene Street.

The tunnel began to turn upward and we could no longer see the light from the basement behind us. I don't know why but we talked in whispers. This was a real thrill—not only had we found something no one knew existed but we were also actually going inside it. Perhaps we were the first people to be in the tunnel in over one hundred years. It seemed like we had walked a long way, and we considered that maybe the tunnel didn't go to the Governor's Mansion but actually went somewhere else. Suddenly, we came to the end of the tunnel. There was a wooden ladder there built into the wall. The ceiling opened up to a small recess.

I put my foot on the ladder and tested it. It seemed strong enough to hold me. I went up three steps and had my head and shoulders inside the recess in the brick ceiling. There was a wooden door at the top of the ladder. I pushed at the wooden door but it didn't budge. I found a piece of paper hanging from a rusty nail next to the door.

I brought the paper with me as I came down the ladder. With both our flashlights on the paper we read, "Today is April First. Happy April Fool's Day." I said to Pam, "I guess this means you can't believe everything you read in newspapers, can you?" She replied, "That's for sure! Let's get out of here."

This chapter appeared in the *Baldwin Bulletin* on April 1, 2005—April Fool's Day. There is not, and never has been, a Milledgeville Tunnel. My apologies to the reader.

INDEX

A

Allen, Mae 66
Allen, Mr. 110
Anderson, John W. 101
Arnold, John T. 101
Arnold, Obadiah 31, 101

B

Babb, C.H. 46
Bagley, John 57
Barksdale, Nan 65
Barnes, Cora 17
Barnes, W.H. 43
Barnes, William D. 17
Barrett, Solomon 64
Bass, Benjamin A. 69
Batson, Tabitha 49
Batson, William A. 49
Bayne, Mr. 54
Beckcom, Samuel 82

Beer, Pam 120
Beeson, Dr. Luther 82
Blizzard, Zillfair 99
Bloodworth, Sallie Belle 54
Bonner, Charles 92
Borden, Lizzie 45
Bostwick, James 28
Bothwell, H.T. 69
Bowing, Dave 52
Boykin, George 46
Bragg, Braxton 78
Brannen, Reverend D.W. 53
Breckinridge, William C.P. 68
Brewer, Daniel 69
Broughton, Seth N. 115
Brown, Governor Joseph E. 50, 88, 113
Brown, W.E. 20
Burke, Edmund 115
Butler, David 27
Butler, Mrs. 27
Byron, Conscription Officer 52

C

Calhoun, James M. 87
Callaway, Dr. 64
Candler, Governor Allen D. 70
Caraker, George 64
Caraker, Jonathan (ficticious character) 119
Carnes, N.K. 51
Carr, Edith 65
Case, Charles L. 64
Case, George 64
Champion, J.W. 46
Chandler, J.B. 46
Chappell, Dr. Harris 82
Choice, William A. 85
Cline, Mary 66
Cobb, Howell 115
Collie, Alexander 114
Colquitt, Governor Alfred H. 29
Combes, J.N. 51
Cook, Samuel A. 64
Cordon, Reverend M.E.H. 23
Cotting, John Ruggles 81
Coyle, Dr. T. Carlton 83
Croley, Dr. 68
Croley, T.J. 46
Cumming, Julian 100

D

Davis, Jefferson 78
DeGraffenried, Boswell B. 114
Denison, Gilbert 60
Denison, Henry 59
Denison, Huldah 60
DeSaussure, Thomas H. 64
DuBignon, Attorney 29
Dubignon, F.G. 101
Dumas, Pearl 53
Dunn, Forest 69
Durden, Frank 36

E

Edwards, Sheriff 101
Ennis, C.W. 46, 100
Ennis, Erasmus A. "Ras" 98
Ennis, Pleasant T. "Doshe" 98
Ewalt, Joseph 67

F

Finney, Ben 54
Finney, Thomas 93
Finney, W.O. "Bill" 93
Fitzsimons, O.P. 102

G

Gause, Ben 46
Gilmore, Dr. 19
Glenn, Luther J. 85
Gooden, Daniel 18
Gooden, Johnny 19
Grantland, Fleming 59
Grantland, Seaton 59
Green, W.J. 69
Greene, Alfred 46
Grieve, Colonel Miller 30
Gumm, Herman 64

INDEX

H

Hall, Dr. 99
Hall, Dr. Iverson Harris 64
Hall, M.W. 20
Harper, Claude 56
Harper, George 55
Harper, W.B. 64
Harper, W.I. 56
Harris, Dr. 99, 101
Harris, Dr. I.L. 26
Harris, Dr. Iverson Harris Jr. 64
Harris, R.T. 46
Haygood, W.E. 100
Hemphill, Harriet 34
Hemphill, Walter 67
Herty, Captain 30
Hill, Benjamin H. 87
Hill, Daniel Harvey 75
Hill, Daniel Harvey Jr. 79
Hines, Beulah 56
Hood, John B. 51
Howard, J.D. 20
Howell, W.F. 46
Hubbard, Martin 51
Hudson, I.C. 69
Hughes, J.T. 69
Hunnicutt, E.T. 87

I

Ivey, C.L. 69
Ivey, Jim 54

J

Jemison, Edwin 73
Jemison, Robert 73
Jemison, Sam 73
Johnson, Gus 28
Johnson, Mary Ann 34
Johnson, Thomas 33
Johnston, Joseph E. 51
Jones, C.A. 68
Jones, Dr. Lodrick M. 64
Jones, Walter 60
Jordan, Benjamin S. 110
Jordan, Leonidas A. 110

K

Kilpatrick, Judson 50
Kimbrew, Jack 98
King, Reverend R.H. 24

L

Ladd, James Royal 111
Lamar, Marshal 101
Laney, James 98
Lattimer, Captain 30
Lawrence, Jefferson 53
Lawrence, Police Officer 93
Lee, Robert E. 73, 77, 91
Leonard, Reverend Simeon C. 45
Leonard, Smithy Ennis 45
Lumsden, B.D. 98
Lyell, Sir Charles 81
Lyle, Eugenia 35

M

Mapp, Frank B. 64
Mapp, Mary E. 105
Marshal, S. 64
Mathis, Charles 67
McCombs, Colonel 27
McCullar, Lewis 19
Miller, Ada 55
Miller, Robert 55
Mitchell, Mrs. Dr. (C.C.) 43
Moffett, Mrs. 43
Moore, James 98
Moore, Maybelle 66
Moore, Sarah 26
Moran, Dr. Owen F. 46
Murphy, E.C. 27
Myrick, Ben D. 69

N

Newell, Dorothy 65
Northen, Governor W.J. 46

O

Orme, Richard M. 59

P

Palmer, L.F. 69
Perry, Deputy Sheriff 68
Perry, Sara Eva 65
Perryman, Judge 37
Pinson, Reverend W.W. 55
Pottle, Joseph E. 20
Priessnitz, Vincent 83
Prosser, Thomas 69

R

Randolph, Sydney 47
Ratteree 55
Reid, George 56
Richardson, Charles 17
Roberts, Mamie L. 65
Robison, Dr. Winfield 68
Russell, Augustus H. 64
Russell, Chappell 99

S

Sanford, D.B. 29, 101
Scott, Coroner 101
Scott, Jack 19
Seddon, James A. 114
Shaw, Michael 25, 107
Shaw, Ordeoro 25
Sherman, William T. 43, 109, 113, 117
Shinholster, Dr. 101
Singleton, Martha 36
Smith, Solomon 13, 14
Stanley, Bill 93
Stanley, Julian 93
Stembridge, Robert Augustus 64
Stembridge, Sidney J. 64
Stroenecker, Edward 74
Stubbs, Baradel 73
Summers, O.C. 64

INDEX

T

Tefft, Israel K. 61
Temple, Ben 47
Terry, Police Officer 94
Thomas, County Treasurer 101
Thomas, John G. 56
Tinsley, Howard 64
Trinkley, Dr. Michael 118

U

Upshaw, David 18

W

Walker, Sam 64
Webb, Calvin 85
West, P.A. 64
Whelan, Charles 67
Whilden, George 64
Whitaker, Dr. 99
Whitaker, Dr. James M. 64
Whitaker, Gertrude 65
Whitaker, Marie 66
White, Johnnie 55
White, W.J. 100
Whitfield, Attorney 29
Whitfield, Robert 20, 68
Wilkes, Reverend Thomas M.W. 87
Williams, Lewis 46
Wilson, Carlos 56, 64
Wilson, J. Herty 56
Wilson, Mr. 100
Wilson, W.T. 64
Wray, Reverend J.A. 54, 68

Wright, Chauncey M. 64
Wright, Stephen E. 64

Z

Zachry, Abner 35, 36
Zachry, Bertie 36
Zachry, Eugenia 36
Zachry, Guy 36
Zachry, Hattie 36
Zachry, Lilla 36
Zachry, Percy 36
Zachry, Robert 37